Praise for
The Essential Credit Repair Handbook

"America is in crisis. The crisis is spelled D-E-B-T. It starts at home and reaches crescendo in our Capitol. There is a solution, spelled D-E-B-O-R-A-H. Deborah McNaughton is a crisis expert. Each chapter in her book is laser-focused on a specific target. This book is relevant and informational for all stages of our financial life. Choose any personal financial subject—Deborah approaches it with vast experience, wisdom, and grace. This book should be required reading as a primer for our Congress and Senate!"

—Bob Hastings, director of sales, Salem Communications

"From tips on how to repair and rebuild your credit report to increasing your FICO scores, getting out of debt, saving money, and building a budget, Deborah McNaughton has the answers. Do you know how to read your credit report? Do you need to re-establish credit? Do you want to buy a house? Does it even matter? Yes it does! And Deborah McNaughton tells you why in her great book, *The Essential Credit Repair Handbook*. A must-read for everyone in today's topsy-turvy society."

—Terry Lowry, host, *The "What's UP?" Radio Program*

The Essential Credit Repair Handbook

By Deborah McNaughton

CAREER PRESS

Pompton Plains, NJ

THE ESSENTIAL CREDIT REPAIR HANDBOOK
EDITED AND TYPESET BY NICOLE DEFELICE
Cover design by Jeff Piasky
Printed in the U.S.A.

To order this title, please call toll-free 1-800-CAREER-1 (NJ and Can-ada: 201-848-0310) to order using VISA or MasterCard, or for further information on books from Career Press.

CAREER
PRESS

The Career Press, Inc. 220 West Parkway, Unit 12
Pompton Plains, NJ 07444
www.careerpress.com

Library of Congress Cataloging-in-Publication Data available upon request.

Dedication

This book is dedicated to all the readers who have been on a roller-coaster ride with their finances and now have landed on level ground to achieve their future financial goals.

Acknowledgments

So many wonderful people have been involved with this writing project. Cynthia Zigmund, who has been my literary agent for many years, has been my greatest promoter. Without Cynthia, I could not have reached out and touched the lives of people who needed financial knowledge.

The team at Career Press has been unbelievable. Each one of them has had an integral part in making this book a reality. A special thanks goes to Michael Pye for catching the vision of this book and putting the team together to make it happen.

To Kirsten Dalley and Nicole DeFelice, my special editors with whom I worked alongside with, a great big thank-you goes to both. Nicole, your patience and recommendations on putting this book together are especially appreciated. Laurie Kelly-Pye, my sales and publicity director, thank you so much for jumping in and getting a great publicity team together to launch this campaign. To all those involved with this book and not mentioned, just know that I appreciate you all.

Lauren Pickens, who is my right hand gal, you are the greatest. This project was made easier because of your help.

And a special thank-you with hugs to my wonderful husband Hal for his patience and encouragement on making this book a reality.

Disclaimer

This publication is designed to provide accurate and authoritative information. It is sold with the understanding that the publisher and author are not engaged herein in rendering legal, accounting, or other professional services. If legal advice or other expert assistance is required, the services of a competent professional should be sought. Neither the author nor the publisher endorses any product or company listed in this book.

All names of the people in the stories have been changed.

Contents

INTRODUCTION

Nobody wakes up one day expecting their financial security and life to be turned upside down as a result of a job loss, illness, pay cut, or uncertainty in the economy. There could be other things that affected your financial stability, but the crisis is over, lessons have been learned during this time of crisis, and you now have a chance to learn from and undo your mistakes, and focus on a new beginning. What a refreshing goal, and one you can achieve.

In today's society, credit reports and credit scores have been the determining factors in obtaining most types of credit and loans. Credit is a way of life. Without it, you can't qualify for a home, car, credit card, or bank loans.

When credit was easy to obtain, many people took advantage of using their credit cards, taking equity from their homes, and using lines of credit for purchases as if they were extra paychecks. It was easy to use the credit cards and equity from our homes to purchase luxury things. Some of the money even went toward investments, such as real estate. Were *your* motives wrong? Probably not at the time you made the investments, but again, no one could see the future and expect loss of income or a financial crisis.

The purpose of writing *The Essential Credit Repair Handbook* is to empower and encourage you to get back on track. One of the main objectives of this book is to give you all the tools you need to repair your credit report and increase your credit scores while reestablishing new credit and improving the credit you currently have.

The book will give you information on the areas of credit you need to improve your situation. It is recession-proof.

In Section I, you will learn how to set new financial goals, as well as understand how you got into the situation you are trying to rectify. There are many credit report and credit card myths that will be discussed to clear up any misconceptions.

Section I will also help you reorganize your budget, save money, and get out of debt. This section will be the platform you will need to follow to begin repairing your credit and rebuilding your credit portfolio.

Credit Repair 101 will be discussed in Section II. This section covers credit reporting agencies, reading your credit report, and step-by-step procedures on how to repair your credit report and increase your credit scores. These are key elements you need to know to enhance your credit report and credit portfolio. I also discuss hiring an outside credit repair company versus doing it yourself, as well as credit card and credit repair scams.

Section III will show you ways to reestablish and build up your credit after a foreclosure, short-sale, bankruptcy, or loan modification. You may have felt all was lost when you experienced these situations, but it is not. One of the main dreams people have is homeownership. You may feel that your dreams have been shattered because of your past credit report. This section will show you how to apply for a home loan, as well as credit cards. You will learn what lenders are looking for during the qualification process. With a solid game plan, you will be able to achieve these dreams.

In Section IV, you will learn the importance of establishing credit in your own name. It also will teach women what they need to know to establish credit in their own name (whether married or single), as well as how they are protected by the law. Couples who are facing a divorce will learn how to get their credit and finances in order before and after the divorce is final.

Knowing credit card laws and protecting your identity is essential. Section IV will discuss those laws as well as identity theft, not only with your credit report and credit cards, but also your medical records.

It is important that you understand how the credit system works and how to protect yourself in the future.

As you read through each chapter, you should come away feeling optimistic about your financial situation. You have a new set of goals, and a road map to reach every one.

This will not be an overnight process, but with careful planning and taking the necessary steps and discipline, I have no doubt that you can achieve all that your heart desires.

SECTION I:

BUILDING YOUR PLATFORM

1

SETTING NEW FINANCIAL GOALS

Times have changed from the good old days when you felt as though you had set good, solid financial goals. You may be one of the survivors of a bad economy that left you with a drop in income and your world turned upside down. Your financial situation may be something that was totally out of your control and had nothing to do with the economy. The financial goals you had previously set were either diminished or set on the back burner.

The good news is that you are back and ready to undo any damage from your past and start a new beginning. It's not easy trying to regroup and get back on top, but you can do it. Stepping back and reassessing your financial goals is a must.

John and Cindy's Story

John and Cindy had been married for more than 10 years. They both had good, stable jobs. Life seemed to be going well. John and Cindy owned a home, had two luxury cars, purchased real estate they used as rentals when the market was booming, and had a nice savings account set aside for emergencies. Never in their wildest dreams did they ever think their life would be turned upside down.

Late one spring, John was laid off from his job. He worked in sales and the office he was working for was downsizing. Although Cindy still had her job, her salary wasn't enough to pay all their bills.

It wasn't long before their savings dwindled down to almost nothing. They had maxed out their credit cards and weren't able to continue making their credit card payments. Soon their mortgage payments started to fall behind, and they eventually lost their home in foreclosure.

After nine months of unemployment, John found another job. It didn't pay as well as his previous one, but he was satisfied being back to work. He and Cindy basically had to start from the bottom to repair their financial situation.

John and Cindy's fear was that they could never get back on track. The lofty goals they had made years ago to have a luxurious life were now substituted with goals of getting out of debt and being able to live within their means. Their priorities changed, and now they had an opportunity to rebuild their financial situation.

Their short-range goals were to get out of debt, live within their budget, and rebuild and repair their credit report. It would take time, but they could do it, and then aim for their long-range goal, which would be to purchase another home.

Goal-setting has changed for most people. Your priorities have changed and although those big goals and dreams are still on your list, they are repositioned to another level in the future.

Many of us have written down our goals, such as buying a home, saving for retirement, paying off student loans, taking vacations, starting a business, and so forth. These are great goals, but are long-range. Most of the time, these are things people will write down as their financial goals. But times have changed. The short-range goals need to be addressed in order to reach the long-range goals.

Rebuilding your credit portfolio includes strengthening your credit report, budgeting, living within your means, and controlling your spending.

Short-Range Goals

Setting goals for your credit and financial needs is just as important as setting goals for your life. As you accomplish each goal, you will gain confidence in setting new ones.

You need to determine how your short-range goals will help you position yourself for the long-term goals. Let's review the short-range goals that will be your building blocks for a great financial future.

- ✓ **A solid budget.** Everyone hates a budget, but if you want to be successful in reaching your financial goals, you must have a workable budget. You need to tighten up your budget so you can save money for your future.
- ✓ **Getting out of debt.** For some people, this is a New Year's resolution. To be successful, you need to eliminate your debt so you can use that money for your long-range goals.
- ✓ **Paying your bills on time.** Sounds easy, but if you get sloppy at paying your bills and they fall behind, your

credit report will be affected and your credit score will decrease.

✓ **Saving money.** Putting money into a savings account will help you achieve your goals.

✓ **Having a good credit report.** It is important that you have a good credit report to achieve some of your long-range goals. Your FICO score is derived from what your credit report says.

✓ **High FICO scores.** High credit scores are a must. Qualifying for most large purchases, such as a home or automobile, will be based on the credit score on your credit report. This should be a high priority on your list.

If you are able to achieve these short-range goals, you will be in a better position to make major purchases. After reviewing your income, net worth, what you can afford with your debt-to-income ratios, and your credit scores, you can see whether these purchases will fit into your budget. Once you have accomplished this, you can move toward your long-range goals.

Long-Range Goals

Most long-range goals constitute some type of investment, luxury item, or type of credit that you want to acquire. As you review these different goals, most of them can only happen once you have accomplished your short-range goals. It is important that you accomplish the short-range goals to further your financial gain.

Review the following long-range goals that most people have, and the basics of accomplishing them.

✓ **Home.** A home is probably the largest investment an individual will ever make in his or her entire life. In order to qualify for a home mortgage or equity line of credit, you must be credit worthy. Without a good credit history and high credit scores, you will not be able to qualify for a home loan. If your credit score is too low, you may not qualify for the best interest rate and terms, or you may be disqualified altogether. Having a high credit score is a must in qualifying for a mortgage approval and low interest rates. The less debt you owe, the higher your credit score will be.

✓ **Automobile, boat, or motor vehicle.** Most people need an automobile or some type of vehicle for transportation. In order to qualify for a motor vehicle, the lender or bank is looking at your FICO credit score. The interest rate and terms the lender will offer you will be based on your credit report score. The higher the credit score, the lower the interest rate will be.

Occasionally, finance companies will let you establish credit if you've never had credit, or if you've had negative credit. For this type of scenario, the cost of the loan and interest rates are substantially higher. An automobile purchase is probably the second-largest investment you will make. If you cannot pay cash for the automobile, try to pay the loan off as quickly as possible.

✓ **Business.** Your goal may be to start or purchase your own business. Establishing a line of credit for a business is frequently needed. A line of credit may be necessary for the start-up of the business or to have on hand for future reserves. This can be done through your bank or a large credit line with a credit card.

When applying for a line of credit, one of the main things banks are looking for on your application is your credit report. If you are unable to qualify for a bank loan, or decide not to apply for a loan, you can use your credit cards as a line of credit for cash advances, but the interest rates are usually higher. By using the line of credit from your credit card, you can request an increase of your credit limit, provided the account is current and in good standing.

✓ **Student loan.** With the rising cost of college, many students need financial aid, which usually involves student loans. Many banks offer students special financial programs. Many of these programs are government loans, which students can defer making payments on until several months after they graduate or leave school. The interest rates are usually low. If you have a child entering college, you may have to qualify for a student loan. Having a good credit report is necessary.

✓ **Retirement.** Although saving for your retirement does not involve your credit report, it does involve being able to save and manage your money. It is important that you have a strong budget in place and stick with it during your retirement days.

As a retiree, you have worked hard to get to this place in life, but you need to make sure that you are able to live comfortably without any financial stress. Staying out of debt is one way to manage your money.

✓ **Investing.** There are many different types of investing. If you are investing in real estate, most of the time you will need to get a loan for the property. A loan for an investment property is more challenging to qualify for. Your credit scores must be high enough, and a substantial down payment and cash reserves are required.

If you are investing in other things such as stocks, bonds, mutual funds, and so on, you must have cash. Being able to budget and save will help you build your financial portfolio.

Goal-Setting Tips

You need to evaluate what it is you want and do everything possible to make your goals a reality. Doing your homework and setting a plan of action can make the goal much easier to accomplish.

Setting goals is time consuming and something most people don't look forward to doing. Procrastination is what usually turns a great idea for goal-setting into a less-than-enthusiastic reality. Goal-setting is your road map to making something happen. It gives you a direction on how you are going to achieve it. You need to follow through and set your sights on goals that are reachable. Careful planning and being responsible will give you a boost toward building a successful financial and credit portfolio.

There are several steps in making goal-setting for credit and financial needs a success. Defining in what areas you may need credit and financial assistance is a must. Review the list of goals mentioned previously. Are these goals you want to accomplish?

When setting your goals, you must be specific. You need to create a Master Financial Goal Worksheet. List the types of things you want to achieve. For example, if it is a home loan, list "mortgage" and the amount you need to qualify. If it is an automobile or other motor vehicle, list the amount you want to finance. If it is for a student loan, list the amount. If you are trying to get out of debt, list the amounts you need to pay off.

You need to be cautioned not to set unrealistic goals that will cause you to be overextended. Make sure the amount of income you bring home can support your household.

10 Steps to Goal-Setting

✓ **Step 1.** Put it in writing.

✓ **Step 2.** Visualize your goal.

✓ **Step 3.** Set a realistic time frame to accomplish the goal.

✓ **Step 4.** Write out your plan of action.

✓ **Step 5.** Remove the excuses you have for not following through with your goal.

✓ **Step 6.** Anticipate any situation that may arise that will cause you to stop moving ahead. If you know of anything in your credit portfolio that could cause you a problem, find a way to correct it. This could be revealed to you through an updated credit report.

✓ **Step 7.** Define your motives. Are your intentions to build a credit portfolio for the future, or only for material gain?

✓ **Step 8.** Look at all your past experiences. Learn from them. Do not be afraid of failure.

✓ **Step 9.** Believe in yourself. You can accomplish what you set out to do.

✓ **Step 10.** Avoid procrastination. Become a doer, not just a talker.

A short-range goal will give you more confidence to reach the long-range goals. Goals will save you time and give you enthusiasm to start your day. Everybody looks forward to new challenges. A good credit and financial portfolio is something that you will live with for the rest of your life.

There is a proverb that says, "Plans fail for lack of counsel, but with many advisers they succeed" (Proverbs 15:22 NIV). If you need advice from a credit or financial expert, don't be afraid to ask for it. You must have knowledge in credit and financial matters. It is a necessity of life.

2

NO REPEAT PERFORMANCES, PLEASE

As you step back and reassess your financial situation, it is time to look back at your past mistakes. So often when we have come through a stressful situation, we tell ourselves, "Never again. I have learned my lesson."

Sounds good, but the problem is that most of us are creatures of habit. We might get beat up along the way, but when we bounce back, it is easy to slowly fall back into making bad choices.

In order to make a full recovery, you need to get to the root of your problem. Why did your credit and finances get out of sync? You need to figure this out as you work on cleaning up your credit report, establishing new credit, and setting new financial goals.

Sometimes you have to take a step back and look as far back as your childhood. Maybe that seems strange to you, but it is not unusual for adults to duplicate their parents' spending habits. For example, if you were living in a home where you saw your parents whipping out the plastic for most of their purchases, it probably looked like free money. Or you may have lived in a home where your parents were very frugal and you had to beg for something you wanted.

Most parents do not discuss their finances with their children, especially if they are having financial difficulties. In essence, if your parents were living off of credit, they probably never discussed being in debt or money management, so in your mind, everything was fine. Why not do what they did?

The example of frugality could point you in one of two directions: You will be frugal as well, or you will become a "credit card spender" and wind up in debt. All of a sudden, you were handed a credit card and you didn't have to ask anyone's permission to buy something. This would be best described as a "power card spender."

Interesting enough, in most marriages, there are two different spending characteristics. One spouse is usually frugal and the other spouse is a spender. It can be frustrating for both if they can't come to a meeting point in handling their finances. Money problems are one of the main reasons people get divorced.

You need to know where your weaknesses are and break those old habits. Listed are several weaknesses that people need to change in order to be successful with a fresh start.

Give It to Me Now

Like so many people who have dealt with past credit problems, it all started with the instant gratification urge. You may have seen or heard an advertisement on something you just had to have. Maybe you were out shopping and saw a flat-screen television with all the bells and whistles, and whipped out your charge card to make the purchase. It may have been a designer handbag. Whatever it was, you had to have it and you made the purchase without thinking about how long it would take you to pay it off and how much the interest was going to cost you.

The days of instant gratification have to be over in order to succeed with a new financial beginning. If you feel the urge to make a purchase and know that it is on an impulse, walk away. Go home and sleep on it. By morning, you should be over the urge. Remember that everything you do with your money has to fit into your budget and able to be paid for with cash. Anything that you do with credit is going to be reflected on your credit report and history.

Living Beyond Your Means

The average person or family lives beyond their means. In other words, you have more bills than you have money to pay them. Credit cards become the source of purchases that you never would have made if you were paying with cash. Credit cards are a false paycheck and give people a false sense of security.

Now that you are beginning fresh with new financial goals, it is important to know what your debt-to-income ratio is. A debt-to-income ratio is a calculation that determines what percentage of your income is going out to pay off debt. For many people, the debts are higher than the income.

To determine what your debt-to-income ratio is, divide your monthly gross income (before taxes) into your total monthly debt. The answer will show your percentage. Here is some basic information on how a credit grantor looks at your application.

When credit grantors look at your application for credit, they will estimate your net income at 80 percent of your gross income (before taxes). Rent or mortgage and bills should not exceed 70 percent of your net income. Other variable expenses such as food, utilities, gas, and so on are estimated to be about 20 to 25 percent of your net income. After the credit grantors assess your income and expenses, they look to see that approximately 90 to 95 percent of your net income is utilized for all your expenses. Anything greater means that you are probably overextended on your credit and debts.

Are You a Charge Card Addict?

Do you have problems walking way from a great sale? How about watching your neighbor buy new things that you want too? Did you ever feel that you are owed this purchase? If you answered yes to these three questions, you need to reverse your thinking. You are still living with your old mindset.

Probably more than half the things we purchase with credit are on an impulse. You may have heard of a great sale that you need to go to. When you arrive at the store, your head may be spinning because there are such great buys.

The old you would load up the shopping cart with items you think you can't live without. After all, it is on sale. You don't have the cash, so you take you credit card and charge it. Once you get your purchases home, you may feel a sense of guilt, because you know that you really didn't need these items in the first place and bought them on an impulse.

The new you must not fall into the temptation of impulse buying. Remember, you just need to walk away and go home. Better yet, don't put yourself in that position to have to walk away. Just don't go to the store where you are tempted. Many people are "sale addicts." Buying on sale is great if you really need the item, but in most instances, the sale purchase is a "want item" and if purchased with a credit card, adds to your debt load.

Keeping Up With Your Neighbor

Keeping up with the Smiths should never be a reason to make impulsive purchases. You have no way of knowing if the Smiths paid cash or used credit to make purchases. Because you don't want to feel as though you are being left behind, you may make a purchase that you really can't afford. Again, you use your credit card or line of credit to make the purchase. Look at what you just did. You just stepped back into the debt trap.

The new you should just be happy for your neighbor and not feel you need to keep up. Things that you don't need will depreciate in value the moment you leave the store, and you are left with a bill that accumulates interest and finance charges.

Sticking Your Head in the Sand

One major problem people have with handling their money is never tracking their spending. This will be discussed in more detail in Chapter 4. The old you never tracked your spending, balanced your checkbook, or recorded your credit card purchases. The term "budget" was a foreign word. It was easy to stick your head in the sand and deny there were any problems.

One of the main things you need to do on your road to financial recovery is to know what is happening with your money and finances at all times. By being in denial and not paying attention to where your money is going, you may suddenly get a wake-up call that you are in worse financial shape than you thought.

With your desire to rebound from your past mistakes, you always need to be on top of your finances and spending.

The Big Deal

Have you ever said to yourself, "When this big deal happens, I will be able to make all this money and can pay everything off?" If you haven't said it, you may know someone that lives with this hope.

Part of your financial challenges may have been from that thinking. You may have invested your money in real estate that went under. It may have been a business or job that made you grandiose promises, but didn't work out. It may have been that stock investment that failed. Whatever the promise or expectation is, you should never spend your money with those assumptions.

It is easy to lose focus on the reality of your true financial position by waiting for the big deal. Many people continue to spend their money and use their credit cards, even with signs that they are going under financially.

The big deal is like a carrot being dangled in front of you. It's easy to keep reaching for it and lose sight of your direction. Never depend on the big deal to make something happen. You need to live in the here and now. Analyze your financial situation today, not what it *may* be in the future when the big deal comes in. Not all big deals happen, and you may have been living with a false sense of security.

By living in the here and now, you can watch your money and spending. Pay your bills as if you never heard of a big deal. Look at the big deal as the icing on a cake, or a wonderful reward, but not as a paycheck.

Jan and Paul's Story

Jan and Paul had been married for several years. They found themselves in a financial dilemma that almost destroyed their marriage.

Both Jan and Paul had spending problems. Jan loved shopping and was an impulse buyer. When she heard about a sale going on at her favorite stores, she made it a point to be there. As she went through the sale racks, she would make impulsive purchases just because the items were on sale, and she would use her charge card to make them. Jan never kept track of her purchases and soon became overloaded with credit card debt.

Paul loved buying electronic gadgets. If it wasn't a new computer and accessories, it was an upgraded cell phone or big-screen television. He was hooked. His purchases were made with a credit card or line of credit. Tracking his charges was never a thought.

Both Jan and Paul had jobs. Unfortunately, Paul's company was downsizing and he was laid off. Reality struck them both when they finally sat down and analyzed their financial situation. It looked pretty grim. They had accumulated high credit card debt, plus they had house and car payments, as well as all their other bills. Taking a step back and assessing their past spending habits was a wake-up call.

Credit counseling was their best resource for help and guidance on how to handle their situation. It was obvious that many of the bills could not be paid on time, so a plan was devised on which bills to pay first. The obvious was their mortgage, food, and utilities. Any money left over would be disbursed to the other creditors.

After six months of unemployment, Paul got another job. Because most of their bills had fallen behind, it was going to be an uphill battle to catch up. Their credit report was bad because of all the delinquencies listed.

As the months went by, Jan and Paul started to get back on track. They also remembered what got them in the situation they were coming out of and were determined to change their old spending habits.

It wasn't easy because the temptation was always there, but they remembered the damage that was done to their credit report and finances. With practice, they both were able to avoid the sales and impulse buying with their new financial goal of repairing their credit report.

Acceptable Debt Calculations

There are calculations that can show you what you can comfortably afford. Most people can afford to pay 10 percent of their net income towards installment debt, not including mortgage payments.

If you find that you are paying more than 15 percent of your net income towards installment debt, you need to cut back. As the percentages go up and you are paying out 20 percent towards installment debt, you are in trouble and need to stop using credit immediately; at 25 percent or more, you are in deep trouble, and need to seek professional help and change your lifestyle.

The best way to make sure that you don't find yourself in over your head in debt is to make sure you calculate these ratios at least once a month.

3

11 MYTHS OF CREDIT

We are living in a world saturated with information. It is not hard to believe that there are many myths and misconceptions causing confusion to many who are searching for answers to their credit and financial needs. There is always the person who heard something from a friend of a friend, and relayed that information to you, making him or her an instant financial expert. Or perhaps you caught the tail end of that radio or television show about credit issues, and it confused you. Whatever it is, you can rest assured that you may have gotten bad information.

There is much confusion regarding areas of credit and credit reports. Listed are 11 myths and misconceptions that will be addressed to clear up the questions you may have.

Myth 1: You should close unused credit cards to increase your credit score.

That may have been true in the past, but not anymore. Years ago, closing unused credit cards was preached. That all changed when FICO credit scores came into existence.

Now, the older your credit cards are, the higher your score will be. In fact, sometimes when you close an older card, you can actually cause your credit score to go down.

The best scores go to people who use credit moderately over a long period of time, so the older the cards, the better. If you need to close some accounts, close the most recent ones that you have opened so that you can keep the cards with the oldest history reflecting current payments. Having no credit history is just as bad as having a bad credit report. Without a credit history, you'll find it very hard to get a major loan when you need one.

Credit scores are tabulated as a result of a "utilization ratio." What that means is that your total debt (balances owed) is calculated as a percentage of all the credit limits of your accounts. If you lower your available credit limits by closing cards, your utilization rate can look higher and hurt your credit score.

Myth 2: You must pay off your credit cards in full each month to increase your score.

Many people think that they must have a zero balance on all their credit cards to get a good score. This is not true. Your credit score is based on the percentage of what your credit balance is to the credit limit. For example, if you have credit limit of $3,000 on one of your credit cards, and your balance was $2,900, your balance to the credit limit of $3,000 is too high and would lower your score.

If you only pay cash for your purchases, there won't be any credit activity on your credit report. It is the payment history that will trigger activity on your credit report.

The ideal way to use your credit is to not charge more than 30 percent of your credit limit. Preferably, you want to keep your balances between 10 and 20 percent (or less) of the credit limit. For example, if you have a credit limit of $1,000, you should keep your balance to less than $200. By doing this, you will show the credit reporting companies that you know how to use your credit wisely and that you make your payments on time.

Myth 3: As long as I make my monthly minimum payment, I am fine.

No you are not fine! If you only make the minimum payment on your account balance, you are accruing interest and finance charges, as well as increasing the time it will take to pay back the credit. Every month that you carry a balance, interest is charged against the unpaid balance. Think of it this way: You took your family on an overnight vacation. You spent one night at a hotel and ate three meals out. This mini-vacation was charged on your credit card.

If you only paid the minimum payment each month, it could take you years to pay off because of the interest and finance charges added each month to your unpaid balance. The majority of the minimum payment is interest. There is only a small amount of your minimum payment that applies towards your principal balance.

Not being able to pay more than your minimum payment each month can keep you in debt for many years. Most of us never think about the possibility of losing a job or a sudden illness, which can hurt our finances. Being in debt will only make matters worse for you.

If you can only make the minimum payment, try adding an additional $5 or $10 to your payment. Just by doing that, you can cut years off your balance and reduce the interest charges that you will incur.

Myth 4: Too many inquiries can hurt my score.

This can be viewed as both true and false. There was a time that this was a true statement, but once the credit-scoring system evolved, it was able to track the type of inquiries made based on the company that requested it.

In other words, if you are shopping for a home or automobile loan, the system would recognize this. If there were several inquiries made within a 14-day window, it will not be held against you.

On the opposite side of this, if you were applying for credit cards or other types of credit on a continuous basis, let's say within a three- to six-month period, it could lower your credit score. How many points? No answer! Credit scoring is top secret. No one knows the point valuation for any item on your report. Interesting enough, if you have your credit report run with any of the three major credit reporting agencies (Experian, TransUnion and Equifax), and you request your credit score, your credit score can drop if there were excessive inquiries. If excessive inquiries are a factor, it will be notated by the credit reporting agency that ran the report.

The best way to avoid excessive inquiries is to get a copy of your credit report from all three of the credit reporting companies before you make a purchase. By ordering your own credit report directly from the credit reporting agencies, you are not penalized. This is called a "soft pull" inquiry and there is no ranking. It will only have an impact if you go to an outside lender or merchant.

Myth 5: Any type of credit is bad.

Not all credit is bad. Credit should only be used for convenience, emergencies, and establishing a credit payment history on your credit report. A big ticket item may be a student loan or mortgage.

If you are using your credit cards as a convenience or emergency because you didn't have the cash when you were making a purchase, that is fine. The trick is to be sure you have the money or resources to pay it off as soon as possible. This will be reflected on your credit report, which will help build your credit history and increase your credit score.

In most cases, student loans and mortgages are investments for your future. When people decide to further their education, generally it is to increase their future income. A student loan may be the only way they can accomplish this. Student loans generally have low interest rates. Once the student graduates, his or her earning capacity should be higher and he or she needs to begin making payments on time.

Investing in real estate with a mortgage should also help you build financial equity. Real estate has its ups and downs, but if you sell when the market is up, you can make a profit with the equity that has built up.

Myth 6: Why bother trying to get myself out of this financial mess? I obviously can't seem to handle my finances.

Rest assured, you're not alone in your financial troubles. Your intention was not to create this debt, but you need to face reality. Learn from your past mistakes and own up to your actions. The debt is yours and no one else's, so you need to come up with a plan to remedy the situation. You will come out of this and restore your good name, but it will take time. Don't lose sight of the end result.

Most of us never learned the proper way of handling our finances from school or our family. Sometimes lessons are learned the hard way. Now it's up to you to accept your situation, learn from your experience, and move on. Make it a point to educate yourself about financial management so that you never find yourself in this situation again. You can get yourself out of this mess and you are capable of handling your own finances.

Myth 7: Co-signing for a friend or family member will not affect my credit report.

Any time you sign an agreement to co-sign for someone else, you are agreeing to pay back the credit. It doesn't matter who you are co-signing for. Once your signature is on the contract, you have a liability in making the payments on time until the balance is paid off. The lender is only agreeing to extend credit to the borrower because you are accepting the responsibility for the borrower's inability to be approved for credit on his or her own. You are basically guaranteeing the loan.

When the loan is complete, the creditor will begin reporting the loan or line of credit on both the co-signer's and borrower's credit report. If the borrower falls behind in making the monthly payments, it will be reported on the credit reports of both borrowers.

Most co-signers sign for car loans for their sons or daughters. Sometimes it may be another relative. If the car payment becomes delinquent or repossessed, severe damage is done to the credit reports of all parties. The co-signer may have problems trying to secure credit for his or her own personal use in the future if there are negative items on his or her credit report. Credit scores will be lowered as well.

Co-signing can carry serious consequences if ground rules are not set in advance. If you decide to co-sign for a loan, or already have, make sure that you get a copy of the billing statement each month to make sure the payments are current. If they are not, you may have to step in and make the payment in order to save yourself from a negative credit rating.

Myth 8: I don't need to worry about my credit. If things really get bad, I can always file for bankruptcy.

With that mindset, bankruptcy is just a cop out. Bankruptcy is a serious matter. You should only consider filing for bankruptcy as a last resort.

It is not as easy to file for bankruptcy as you may think. You will have to go through financial counseling first. An outline of your budget, including your income and expenses, will be reviewed by a court-appointed trustee to determine if you are eligible for a Chapter 7 bankruptcy that discharges your debts, or a Chapter 13 that will put you in a reorganization program to pay back your debts. Either way, the bankruptcy entry will be on your credit report for up to 10 years.

A bankruptcy becomes a matter of public record. A public record becomes a part of your credit report. A bankruptcy can affect you for a long time whether applying for credit, life insurance, or even some employment positions.

Don't look at bankruptcy as an easy out. Revisit your current financial situation to see what you can do to improve your situation. Use bankruptcy as a last resort only.

Myth 9: Credit counseling will destroy my credit score.

Being in a credit counseling debt management program is not considered negative in the scoring models. Most debt management programs work with you and your creditors to lower you monthly payments.

If you went into a debt management program and you were never late on making payments, the accounts will have a positive history. A debt management program does not report your accounts to the credit reporting agencies. It is the creditor that may or may not report it. At that point, it is up to a credit grantor as to how they will view it. In most instances, unless the credit score is very low, the credit grantor may never look at the credit report and may only rely on the credit score.

On another note, if you went into a debt management program and your accounts were delinquent prior to entering the program, you will already have a low credit score. The best thing that can happen to you is that while in the debt management program, you are able to bring your accounts current, which will reflect a higher credit rating.

Once you have completed the debt management program, your accounts will be paid off and you will have a history of consistent payments that will help you in rebuilding your credit.

Myth 10: Credit scores are locked in for six months.

Credit scores can change anytime there is new activity. When a credit grantor requests a copy of your credit report and credit score, the scores that are calculated and reported are for that day only.

Most merchants report payment history on a monthly basis to the credit reporting agencies. If there is any change with your accounts, such as an increase or decrease of your balance, the score will change. If you have fallen behind in making your payments, the score can decrease. A public notice, such as a judgment or tax lien, can be reported, which will lower your score.

Each time the credit report is rerun, the credit scores will be recalculated and a different credit score can appear if there was any data on your credit report that changed.

Myth 11: Putting a statement in your credit reports can help raise your score.

Although the law says you can add a 100-word statement to your credit report on an entry, it is probably a waste of time. A statement will not have any influence on your credit score other than telling your side of the story.

If you have an entry being reported inaccurately or feel it is not correct, you can dispute this with the creditor or credit reporting agency. It is more difficult to dispute an entry if you have a written statement noted on the credit report. If you decide to dispute an entry, but already have a statement on the report, remove it before you proceed.

4

TIPS FOR AN EFFECTIVE BUDGET

Before you can begin repairing your credit report and reestablishing your credit, you need to be sure your financial problems have been addressed. If you don't, you will only find yourself back in the same situation. Setting up a workable budget is a must. If you owe more than you earn, not only will you never dig yourself out of the mess you're in, but you will also have a difficult time reestablishing your credit.

If you are currently behind in paying your bills, and creditors are still after you, credit repair is not for you at this time. Instead, you need to first get a handle on your bills, and the first step in doing that is setting up a realistic budget.

A Wake-Up Call

Who likes to think about budgeting? For most people, when you mention the "B" word, their eyes glaze over, or a look of panic appears on their faces. Maybe because they are in denial or too afraid to see how out of control their spending really is. Whatever the reason for the instant stress attack may be, setting a budget is a necessity for financial wellness.

You made the decision to set up a budget when you realized your spending was out of control. You found yourself constantly running out of money by the end of the month. You had more bills than money. You have heard that before, but never believed it could happen to you.

A budget is simply a spending plan that includes everything you spend money on based on the amount of your income. It is also a reference tool for you to make sure you are living within your means.

When setting up your budget, you can make it very basic and simple, or more structured and wise. A basic budget would include everything you spend money on that is within your income. A more structured or wise budget would include not only the basics, but also areas for you to set money aside for specific goals, such as savings, giving, investing for your retirement, education, and so on. In the beginning, you may only be able to do a basic budget while trying to get a grip on your spending.

Begin Your Budget Plan

There are two steps that you need to do before you can really get a handle on your spending. This must be done before you create your "real deal" budget.

Step 1: Collect all your income receipts, including pay stubs, deposit receipts, and additional income, such as alimony, child support, and interest dividends.

Review how much your fixed monthly housing expenses are, including rent/mortgage, car payments, utilities, insurance, and taxes. Then list the transportation costs for your vehicles that fluctuate, such as fuel, maintenance, registration, and parking fees. List everything you think you are spending money on monthly: food, medical expenses, child expenses, legal expenses, loans and credit cards, and so on.

Get a notebook, pencil, and a calculator. You can also use a monthly budget calculator on *www.financialvictory.com*.

List all of your income in one column. In the second column, list your expenses. Total the income and estimate expenses. Next, subtract the total expenses from the total income. You will either have a negative or positive number.

Did you notice the word *estimate*? Whatever your number is, it is not the "real deal." You're getting there, but it is just the beginning.

Step 2: *For the next 30 days, write down every nickel, dime, and penny that you spend in your notebook.*

You can not get a true picture of what your budget should look like until you do this exercise. Actually you can't begin to create a workable budget until this is done. You must get a true picture and it will take one to two months. The first step was just a preview of what you thought you were spending.

Name this page "My Spending Journal." This page includes your monthly expenses, including credit card charges, all cash expenditures, trips for fast food, coffee and soda stops, candy bars, magazines, gifts, and so on. Place the items in categories, such as clothes, entertainment, dining out, and so on.

There are a couple of different ways you can do this exercise, such as using Quicken software, that will track your spending using figures from your checkbook and credit card statements.

Your bank may also have a program that you can use online, or there are Websites that can help you track, such as *www.mint.com*.

The main thing to remember is to break down your cash withdrawals and put them in the category that you spend it on. For example, if the $20 you withdrew from the ATM is going for food and a movie, add that to your category.

At the end of the month, total all of the columns. This is definitely going to be a wake-up call for you. For example, you might see you're spending approximately $250 for dining out, $50 for candy bars, sodas, and coffee runs, $100 for electronic purchases, $45 for nails, and so on.

Go back to your budget sheet and create a new monthly budget. Reenter what you have spent money on for the month, including your fixed expenses. Now add your income column and your expenses column. Subtract the total expenses from your total income. The total is the "real deal." These are the things that have caused you to have more bills than money. Don't be too upset! This is the reality check you need to change your financial destination and course. Do this same exercise again for the next 30 days.

Let the Budget Begin

Now that you have done the preliminary work, its time to dig deeper into your past spending. You now have insight on some of your weaknesses after completing your 30-day journal and creating a mock budget.

It's now time to dig deeper. This may be time consuming, but you are getting closer to seeing the true picture. Collect all of your checking, savings, and credit card statements for the last year. Find all of the receipts for any cash purchases. Like most people, you have probably thrown them away. If that is your situation, begin saving all receipts from now on.

Once you have collected the statements and receipts for the past 12 months, make a category for each type of purchase. Total each column separately. Once each column is totaled, add them all together. This is the grand total of all your expenses. Total your income for the past 12 months and subtract your expenses. This is the amount that you have left after everything was paid. How does it look? Do you have a positive or negative number? If it is negative, there still is more work to be done. To break this down into a monthly average, divide the total expenses by 12. This will give you an idea of what your average monthly outflow is.

Review every column of your totaled expenses. Look for ways that you can trim these expenses down. You will need to do the same procedure you did with your monthly journal. For example, if you found you were spending annually $3,600 on clothes, $1,200 on gifts, $3,000 dining out, $2,400 on hobbies, and so on, you can cut back. Just adding these items total $10,200 per year or $850 per month. If you cut back half of this total and put it back into your budget, that would give you an extra $425 per month. That is a savings of $5,100 per year. This is money that you can use to plug the leaks in your budget, apply toward paying off debt, or add to your savings.

Percentage Breakdowns

As you complete your budget, listing the actual expenses and the projected expenses (ones that may change monthly), it is important that you balance your income and spending.

The following is a recommendation of the percentage of income that should go into each category of your budget.

- ✓ **Housing (including taxes and insurance):** 35%
- ✓ **Debt payments:** no more than 10 to 15%
- ✓ **Food (includes eating out/fast food):** 15 to 20%
- ✓ **Transportation (including insurance, fuel, maintenance):** 15%
- ✓ **Other (clothes, healthcare, utilities):** 10 to 15%
- ✓ **Giving/tithing/charity:** 10%
- ✓ **Savings:** 10%

These are only suggested percentages. Each person will have a different scenario based on what his or her debt load is. If there are no credit card payments, you now have 10 to 20 percent more to put in your budget. You are the only one that can disburse your expenses into each category. Don't worry if they are not exact. One category may be higher than what is listed while another category may be lower.

Your basic budget may not seem to have room for savings or giving. Determine what you believe is right for your situation and contribute appropriately. A person building a wise budget will be able to budget for giving and savings along with the other categories.

12 Tips to Make Your Budget Work

Tip 1: When setting up your budget, don't forget to include your "Budget Busters."

A budget buster is an expense that is not billed monthly. It may be an annual, semi-annual, or quarterly expense. An example of this would be property taxes, car or home insurance, automobile mainte-nance, or accountant fees. Review your last 12 months' expenditures. You will be able to spot which expenses were not billed monthly. To put your budget buster expenses into your budget, you need to add the totals and divide the total expense by 12 months. This will break it down into a monthly amount. You need to deposit the amount of the item into a special separate bank account on a monthly basis. When the bill is due, you will already have it saved and ready to pay.

Tip 2: When you review your monthly journal, find areas where you feel your spending is excessive.

This is also an exercise you should do when reviewing your budget. You may be able to increase your deductibles on insurance policies, or change your calling plan on your mobile phone.

Tip 3: Review your expenses to determine if there will be an increase or decrease in your expenses for the next year.

This may include maintenance, insurance, taxes, and so on. Be sure to make the adjustment in your budget.

Tip 4: Open more than one bank account.

If everything is deposited into your checking account, you will have the temptation to spend it. Have one main account to pay your bills, but open a separate account for your budget buster items, such as property taxes, insurance, and so on. Also have a separate account opened for unforeseen emergencies. This could be for a broken water heater, new brakes and tires for your car, medical care if your children get sick, and so on. Having an emergency fund will eliminate using your credit cards for an emergency.

Other accounts could be used for holiday gifts, or a special savings account to make a major purchase. You may not feel like you are at that point of multiple accounts with your budget, but the day will come that you can disburse your extra money into these different accounts.

Tip 5: It is recommended that you have at least three to six months of living expenses saved.

Make that one of your goals. Just putting approximately $167 in saving per month will add up to more than $2,000 in a year.

Tip 6: When paying your bills, your budget should go in the following order:

✓ **Food.** You need food to keep you healthy.
✓ **Utilities.** You need to keep the lights and power on.

- ✓ **Housing (rent or mortgage).** A roof over your head is essential.
- ✓ **Transportation costs (gas, car payment, car insurance).** If you can't get to work, you can't earn any money.
- ✓ **Clothing.** While trying to get your budget under control, clothing should only be purchased out of necessity, not out of want.
- ✓ **Health.** You have to take care of your health. Most of us have co-pays and deductibles to meet, so we need to anticipate those medical payments in our budget.

Once the essential bills are paid, anything left over is called "discretionary income." This is what should be used to pay your credit cards and anything else that remains.

Tip 7: Discuss your budget with your spouse if you are married, or a trusted friend if you are single.

Two heads are better than one. It is important that you are accountable to someone to make sure you are on track with your budget and finances.

Tip 8: Budgets can fail if you are unrealistic on the allocation of your spending.

It is a good idea to overbudget until you get a handle on your true expenditures. For example, if you think you are spending $300 towards groceries every month, add another $100 to the budget. If you were wrong, this extra money will cover you. If you were correct, then you have extra money to allocate towards other expenditures.

Tip 9: Break bad habits.

Many budgets are blown because of bad habits we may have. Whether it's alcohol, smoking, gambling, and so on, the cost can add up and break your budget. Give up any vices that are costing you money and use it toward your budget and to pay down your debts. Not only will you see your debts go down, but your health will improve and you'll save on medical bills as well.

Tip 10: Balance your checkbook and keep your receipts.

Disaster strikes when you don't balance your checkbook. Nowadays it is very difficult because of the use of the ATM and debit cards. It is easy to forget to record your cash withdrawals or purchases in your check registry. By not properly recording your purchase or withdrawal, you may find that you have less money than you anticipated and not be able to stick to your budget. If you are not good at balancing your checkbook, go to your bank's Website and check your balance and debits every few days to make sure you know where your money is going.

As you found when doing your 30-day journal, you were able to account for whatever money you spent per day. You may need to go back to using your monthly spending journal. By doing this, it will make you accountable until you can get in the habit of recording your purchases and spending.

Keeping your receipts will help you get back on track with your budget if you have gone astray. If you forget what you spent your money on, having a receipt will jog your memory to record the transaction.

Tip 11: It is important that you make giving a part of your budget.

Most people have a desire to give or donate money to their church or place of worship, community, or charity. You will reap the rewards of knowing you have helped a needy cause.

Tip 12: Use cash when possible.

By using cash instead of your credit card, ATM or debit card, or a check, you will be able to control your spending and keep your budget intact. Most people will choose to use their credit or debit card rather than cash for a purchase. In many cases, that is how debt begins.

How to Budget Using the Cash Envelope System

The first thing you need to do is take out enough cash to last one week at a time. (If you prefer to put all your cash into each envelope on a monthly basis rather than weekly, you can.) Divide your spending into the following categories: food, gas, clothing, entertainment, and so on.

1. Create an envelope for each category.
2. Fill each envelope with the right amount of money. For example, if your food allowance is $400 per month, divide the $400 by the number of weeks in the month, which would be $100 per week. Label the envelope FOOD and place the $100 in the envelope. Place the allocated weekly cash in each of the envelopes with the designated category.
3. Pay for your purchases out of the appropriate envelopes. For example, use the food envelope only for food purchases, and the gasoline purchase envelope only for gasoline purchases. Once the money is gone in each of the categories, you must stop spending until the next month. No cheating! Don't take money from one category to replace the category that you depleted.
4. If you have any money left over in the envelopes, add this to your savings or use it to pay down some of your debt.
5. Beginning the next month, follow the same procedure as the previous month. Fill each of the envelopes with the designated amounts of cash.

The envelope system will help you stay on track with your budget. The benefit is that you will be able to tweak your spending habits and see your debts go down while keeping within your budget.

5

SAVE MONEY WHILE RETIRING YOUR DEBT

Your head is probably spinning after looking at your budget and seeing the real numbers. Are you a bit concerned? Hang in there, because this chapter is going to show you different strategies on saving money that will help you get out of debt. At the beginning of every new year, one of the top three resolutions is getting out of debt. It may start out as a great idea, but after a couple of months of trying to cut back on their spending, most people give up. That is because they don't have a solid plan on how to get the extra money they need to retire their debt. It doesn't really matter what time of year you set your sights on eliminating your debt. As long as you are only making minimum monthly payments, nothing is going to happen unless you loosen up some extra money.

Make a List

Now that you have put together your budget, you might be feeling very uncomfortable and maybe a bit stressed at the amount of money you are paying out each month. How much of your monthly payments are going toward credit card debt, car loans, bank loans, student loans, medical bills, or any other type of credit you owe?

One of the first things that you need to do when strategizing getting rid of your debt is find out exactly what you owe, and what it is costing you to continue making payments on this debt. This will also help you determine how much you may be short to pay it off.

From your budget sheet and monthly statements from your bills, you must make a list of what is owed. Include the name of the creditor, type of credit, the balance owed, interest rate, and payment. For example:

Creditor	Type of Credit	Balance	Interest Rate	Payment
Simple Bank	Visa	$4,000	29%	$210
Main Bank	MasterCard	$3,200	16%	$139

When you have totaled the debt amount, you may find your-self overwhelmed. You can see the numbers, but don't quite see how you are going to come up with the money to pay your debt off. It's all about finding ways to find money in your budget. It may not be as hard as you think if you are going to be completely honest with what you are spending your money on. There are several ways to cut back on your spending.

Raising Cash to Pay Down Debt

Believe it or not, you do have money at your fingertips that you can raise. It just takes some creativity on your part. Some things may be very obvious to you and some may take sacrifice on your part. Just remember this journey will not take forever. You can do it.

1. **Sell treasures you don't really need that are draining your bank account.** We all have things sitting around our house that have some value, but are not used. Basically they are just gathering dust. If you have items that fit this description, SELL THEM!

❑ Is that extra car or vehicle parked in your yard costing you license fees, registration, maintenance fees, and insurance?

❑ Is your car a gas guzzler?

❑ Do you have old CDs, books, videos, computer games, or toys that you (or your children) have outgrown?

❑ Do you have old cell phones or outdated electronics?

❑ Do you have designer clothes, handbags, or jewelry you never wear?

❑ Are there appliances or furniture stored in your garage or a storage facility that you never use?

❑ Do you have things that you can sell at a garage sale?

Once you have taken inventory of your things, sell them. Apply the money that you make toward paying down your debt. If you have money left over, put it in your savings.

2.　**Use your gifts and talents to make money.**

❑ Work overtime, or take a part-time job. Remember, this is only temporary.

If you are gifted in areas that people are willing to pay you for, do it. For example:

❑ You may be computer literate and can help individuals with their computer needs.

❑ You may have a teaching background and can tutor students. If you have a masters or specialized degree, you may be able to teach at a community college.

❑ You may be good at home decorating or party planning.

❑ You may be good at auto repair. Friends and family are great customers.

❑ You may be good at writing. Many companies are looking for skilled writers.

Everyone has special skills, interests, or hobbies that can make extra money. Look at how many young children sell lemonade on the corner. They are using their skills to raise money and are our future entrepreneurs.

With the extra money you make using your special talents, apply it to your debt. Once your debt is paid off, you may find that you want to continue making extra money doing things that you enjoy.

3. **Use gift and refund money to pay down debt.** Bank the money that you get from your birthday, holiday gifts, work bonus, tax refund, rebates, settlements, insurance refunds, and so on. Use most of that money to pay down your debt. Go ahead and buy yourself something using 10 percent of what you have received. If you don't reward yourself, you will be discouraged, so treat yourself. With the remaining 90 percent, pay down your debt. You will be glad that you did.

4. **Bartering will save you money.** There may be a service that you need and don't have the money to pay for. Find out from the business owner if there is any service that you can provide in exchange. A great example would be that you are in need of a computer repair. You have special skills in automotive. It so happens that the business owner needs some work on his car, so in exchange for you working on the business owner's car, he will repair your computer.

Bartering is a win-win situation for both services. It may not put money in your pocket, but it will save you money.

Month-to-Month Savings

Every month, you have bills that need to be paid. When you evaluate your financial situation, stop and think how you may be able to save money with the essential bills that you are paying. Essential bills that should always be paid first are your rent or mortgage payment, utilities, food, and transportation.

1. **Can I afford where I live?** Many people are paying more on their homes and apartments than they can really afford. It may not have started out that way, but as more and more things are purchased and the debt continues to climb, the debt-to-income ratio increases.

   A good rule to follow on what you can afford is to pay no more than 35 percent of your net income (after taxes) toward housing cost. If you are, it could be time to reevaluate your financial situation. You may need to consider moving to a home or apartment that has lower payments. If this is not an option, then you can advertise for a roommate to rent spare bedrooms and pay you rent. There may be other ways to reduce your costs in another category.

2. **How can I reduce my utility bills?** Your utility bills are essential bills that are a necessity. They are part of the survival bills that you should pay. Gas, water, and electricity are the primary bills. A telephone would also count in this category.

   Ask yourself, can I reduce any of my utility costs? The answer is yes, provided you are consistent.

   ❑ An easy start is to make a conscious effort to turn off your lights and appliances when not in use. That includes your computer.

   ❑ Lower your thermostat by one or more degrees in the winter. Use more blankets and use wood in your fireplace to heat your home.

❑ In the summer months, set your thermostat higher for your air conditioning.

❑ Cut down on your water use by taking shorter showers and avoid running water. When brushing your teeth, don't let the faucet run.

❑ Check for leaky pipes and toilets.

❑ Check with your telephone carrier to make sure you have the lowest rates.

❑ Many people are opting to give up their landlines and only use their cell phones. Compare prices to see what your best option is.

❑ Use your e-mail, Skype, and old-fashioned letter-writing to save on your telephone costs.

❑ Lower your cellular phone bill by getting the minimum minutes. Use your cellular phone only for emergencies.

❑ Cancel the bells and whistles on your home phone for call waiting, three-way calling, and caller ID.

❑ Combine your Internet, cable, and phone service with one carrier.

3. **How can I cut my food costs?** You can't get by without food, but you can save money on what you buy. When you shop for your groceries, go to a grocery store or food warehouse. You can save money several ways. Sometimes even a pharmacy or drug store may have great discounts on their shelves. Milk products have been seen as cheaper at a drug store than the supermarket.

❑ Never go grocery shopping when you are hungry. It's amazing the junk food that is calling your name as you navigate through the aisles.

❑ Shop at low-cost stores, use coupons, and avoid convenience stores.

❑ Pre-packaged foods are more expensive than buying ingredients to make simple, fresh, home-cooked meals.

❑ Buy only items that you use on a regular basis.

❑ Avoid snack and soda vending machines. Carry your own snacks and drinks. If you spent one dollar per day at the vending machine five days a week, in one year you would have wasted $260. And lots of calories, too.

4. **How can I save on automobile and transportation expenses?** If you work outside your home, you need some sort of transportation to get to and from work. Most people don't live close to their jobs, so they depend on their automobiles. In most households there are two vehicles (unless you are single). There are ways to lower your costs.

When trying to calculate what you should be spending on automobile and travel expenses, the rule is to keep your expenses at an average of 15 percent of your net income. Too many people purchase and finance vehicles and end up paying high monthly payments. Remember, as soon as you drive that vehicle off the car lot, the value goes down.

If you are paying a high monthly car or lease payment, and there is not enough equity or value in your car to sell it or turn it in to the car dealer, you need to find ways to offset your payment.

There are some companies that have ride share programs. These companies will pay you money to carpool with other coworkers or take public transportation. If your company doesn't offer this program, find someone that you can carpool with and split the gas money.

If there is bus or subway transportation, you can alternate this with your driving. And nothing is cheaper than walking or riding a bike to work.

❑ Look for the cheapest gas prices.

❑ Take care of your car with regular oil changes, rotating tires, and tune-ups.

❑ If your car is costing you more money in repairs per year than a car payment would, it's time to get another car. It doesn't make sense to keep pouring money into car repairs if it is an older car.

❑ Buy a used car instead of a new one.

❑ Always check with your car insurance agent before making a purchase to see how much your car insurance will go up or down. Your car insurance can break the bank depending on the make and model of your car.

❑ Pay higher deductibles on your auto insurance. This will reduce your premium.

❑ If you are paying a high interest rate on your car loan, shop around and see if you can refinance with your bank or credit union.

5. **How can I save on childcare?** Childcare is an essential cost. If you work outside the home and have children, childcare may be a necessity. If you feel you have found a program that works for you with someone you trust, or a school that you feel is right for your child, stick with it. Look for other ways to cut back. If you have found that your current childcare situation isn't good, you can look for other alternatives as long as you keep your child's welfare protected.

❑ For in-home childcare, contact your church or college. Many churches and colleges have job centers or bulletin boards to help match up people both needing and offering work.

❑ There are many retired seniors looking to help with childcare.

❑ Home-schooled teenagers can be great babysitters.

❑ Swap with a neighbor or close friends for babysitting. Many mothers will take turns babysitting each other's children.

6. **Is there a way to decrease my automobile and homeowner's insurance costs?** In most states, you are required by law to have automobile insurance if you own an automobile. If you are a homeowner, your lender will require you to have homeowner's insurance.

❑ Contact an insurance broker. An insurance broker can shop different companies to get you the cheapest rates.

❑ Look for higher deductibles.

❑ Combine both home and automobile into one insurance policy for lower rates.

7. **Do I really need medical insurance?** Having medical insurance should be a priority. You never know when something can happen to your health. Many companies offer group policies for their employees. When shopping for medical insurance:

❑ Make sure it has the coverage you need.

❑ Do comparative shopping for rates.

❑ Increase your deductible to lower your rate.

❑ Depending on your age, ask your insurance agent about any supplemental medical insurance programs.

❑ Request generic prescription drugs.

❑ Purchase over-the-counter medications when needed.

8. **What if I don't have medical coverage?** There are things you can do if you don't have medical insurance. There are some medical savings programs available that may offset your expenses.

❑ Negotiate with your doctors or healthcare provider to see if they can discount their fees if you pay cash for their services.

❑ Shop prescription cost with multiple pharmacies.

❑ If you need lab work or x-rays, find out how much the fee is without insurance. Many doctors, medical labs, and radiation centers offer discounts for people who don't have insurance.

Other Money-Saving Smarts

As you can see, there are definitely priority items that you can't live without. You may have other things on your list that weren't mentioned. Anything that pertains to survival and necessity must be paid before any other bills. If you can find ways to cut down those expenses, you will have more money to work with on the other items most people fall prey to.

The following list shows the real-life things that ruin most people's budgets. Do you have to go without? Maybe, but let's see how you can compromise and not feel deprived.

1. **Do I have to give up eating out, drinks, and other luxuries?** In order to save money, you may need to cut back on some of the things you like to do. Notice the words "cut back"?

❑ Coffee money. Flavored and gourmet coffee drinks at your favorite coffee shop will cost you. If you spent $3.50 per day on your favorite coffee drinks five days a week, in one year you would have spent $910. That's enough to pay off some of your bills. How many cans of coffee could you have purchased? Bring your own coffee, and opt for one coffee run a week. Put your savings towards your bills.

❑ Limit eating out. Instead of four days a week, make it one or two days. Put the savings aside to tackle your debt.

❑ If you are going out, order water and split meals. Eat before your go, and only order appetizers or a dessert.

2. **Do I have to give up shopping?** Not necessarily! You may need to change the way you shop. Impulsive shopping will drain your bank account. There are ways to shop and save money. Remember, you only want to shop for things you need, not things you want. Saving money should be your goal.

❑ If there is an item you absolutely need to buy, check out the prices at several stores and search the Internet. There are great Websites (such as: *www.Groupon.com*, *www.couponmom.com*, and *www.thecouponclippers.com*) where you can clip coupons, not only for groceries, but for most items.

❑ Take advantage of rebates.

❑ Shop at consignment stores, garage sales, and second-hand stores.

❑ Go to discount stores to get your best buys.

❑ Check your mail and newspapers for grocery discounts each week.

❑ Watch the newspapers for sales at your favorite store.

Random Savings Tips

- ✓ Find a bank that does not charge service fees for your checking or savings account.
- ✓ When visiting an ATM machine, make sure it is affiliated with your bank to save you any additional charges. This can save you up to $2.50 per transaction.
- ✓ Drop your gym and health club memberships. Exercise at home or with a friend. Invest in workout DVDs.
- ✓ Get your news from the Internet, television, or radio, as opposed to buying daily newspapers.
- ✓ Save money by visiting your library, and reading free articles on the Internet. Borrow free DVDs from the library.
- ✓ Avoid purchasing warranties.
- ✓ Review your television cable bill to see what you can cut out.
- ✓ Get store reward cards and use them.
- ✓ Invest in power strips for your entertainment center and home computer.
- ✓ Review credit card statements each month to make sure there are no fraudulent charges.

6

GET OUT—AND STAY OUT—OF DEBT

Don't throw in the towel yet! You probably are feeling that this is getting to be too much work, but it's not. By doing the preliminary exercises with your budget analysis, money tracking, and finding ways to save money, you're now ready to tackle your debt and start seeing results. All you need are different strategies to help you get there.

The first thing you need to do is stop using your credit cards! Use cash, checks, or debit cards (don't forget to write it down in your register). That seems so obvious, but you would be surprised at how many people start a plan to get out of debt and are still racking up the charges on their credit cards each month.

Let's walk through several different strategies and scenarios to help you get rid of your debt once and for all.

Basic Things to Do

Call Your Credit Card Company

A simple call to your credit card company asking them to reduce your current interest rate should always be the first thing that you do. It may not always work, but if you have been on time with your payments and have a long history with their company, they may do it. They may ask if you are facing a financial hardship. If you feel the interest rate is too high and causing you to struggle, answer yes. If you are not facing a financial hardship, find out if they are willing to lower the interest rate anyway.

If the company does agree to lower your interest rate, your monthly payment would be lowered, too. They may, however, close your account. Make sure you weigh all the facts that they give you before making your decision. It doesn't hurt to try, and it doesn't cost anything. If they do close your account, you will not be able to charge anymore. That is not all bad because you are trying to eliminate your debt! It could affect your credit score though, which will be discussed in Chapter 10.

Balance Transfers

Balance transfers can reduce your interest rates and finance charges, and save you money. If you have a credit limit that has not been maxed out, you may be able to transfer your high interest rate credit cards to your lower interest rate cards.

The 0-percent interest rates or other low rate cards that offered teaser rates may be extinct. If you do find a credit card offering those terms, you need to know the details. Most of the low interest rate cards are for a specified period of time, and will eventually go up. Read the fine print on their disclosures. Check to see if there is a transfer fee. If there is a significant savings, go ahead and do it.

Review all of your credit cards. If you have two credit cards, one may have a credit limit of $10,000, an interest rate of 14 percent, and a balance of $1,200. Your second credit card has a credit limit of $3,000, an interest rate of 21 percent, and a balance of $2,500. Transfer your credit card balance of $2,500 with the 21 percent interest rate to the credit card with the 14 percent interest rate. You would now owe $3,700 on the credit card with the 14 percent interest rate. You have saved 7 percent interest.

The secret to making this work is to add the payment that you had been making on the credit card with the 21 percent interest rate to the payment you would make on the credit card with the 14 percent interest rate. This way, you will be able to save money on the interest and finance charges by paying the lower interest rate. Another benefit is there is more money applied toward the principal balance that would allow you to pay the debt off sooner. The key to making this work and getting you out of debt is to not charge anything else to the account you have transferred.

Make Extra Payments

Adding extra money to your minimum payment will reduce your principal balance. As the principal balance goes down, you will be able to retire that debt in record speed.

Have you ever really looked at the amount of interest you are paying on your credit cards each month, as well as each year? Have you ever tried to calculate how long it will take to pay off your credit card debt?

For example, you have a credit card with a $2,000 balance and an interest rate of 21 percent. If you were to make only the minimum payment and never use the card again, it would take you more than 16 years to pay off, and the interest that it would cost is more than $2,500. If you add that to the balance of $2,000, the total that you paid for this one card and purchases would be $4,500.

If you can't increase your minimum payment by much, try adding $5 or $10 extra per month to the payment. This would reduce the amount of time needed to pay off the balance as well as save you in interest charges.

Set an Annual Amount Toward Your Estimated Payments

One major mistake people make when trying to pay down their debt is paying the minimum payment plus extra, but not being consistent with the payment. The way the credit card companies calculate the payment is based on a percentage of the balance. As your credit card balance goes down, so does the minimum payment. If you lower your payment each month based on the new minimum amount due, it still is adding years to your debt. Set an amount you can pay each month and stay consistent with it, regardless of the lower minimum payment. If your minimum payment is $75 and you can add $100 more to it each month, totaling $175, stay with that amount until you pay it off.

The best way to pay all of your credit cards off is to review and total all your credit card payments for the past 12 months. Total this amount and divide that amount by 12 (months). That is the amount you want to continue to pay each month. Don't decrease it.

For example, if your annual worksheet totaled $6,000 per year of credit card payments, divide $6,000 by 12 months. The total is $500 per month. This is the amount you would continue to pay monthly. As each balance is paid off, apply the excess to whatever credit card you are focusing on paying off first. Once you have paid off each of your debts, put the extra money in your savings.

Unpeeling the Debt Layers

Looking at your credit worksheets, you are probably viewing layers of credit card debt ranging from high balances to low balances. Some credit cards have high interest rates, while others have low interest rates. Credit experts don't agree on which to pay first. This is a personal decision.

Before you make your decision on what to pay first, ask yourself, what keeps you more motivated? Is it seeing faster results and giving yourself a gold star, or having things move more slowly? Either way, you need to reward yourself once you have paid off your debts. Most people like to see faster results and opt for the lower balances to pay off first.

One of the strategies used with this technique is called the "Snowball Effect."

Make a list beginning with your high-balance credit cards down to the lowest-balance card. List the company name, balance, and monthly payment. This example illustrates paying off the lowest balances first.

Company	Balance	Payment
ABC Company	$2,900	$125
KPP Company	$1,500	$100
Alpha Credit Card	$1,200	$80
May Dept. Store	$600	$20
Bloom Dept. Store	$250	$15

As you begin paying off each card, starting with the lowest balance, take the payment that you would be making to the lowest balance and add it to the next credit card balance you are trying to pay off. For instance, the balance of $250 had a payment of $15. Once you pay this off, add the $15 to the minimum payment on the next balance of $600, and continue doing this until it also is paid off. Then take the two payments you were making on the department stores and add it to the next balance in addition to the minimum payment. Continue this strategy until all the credit cards are paid off. You are peeling off layers of your credit card debt, one card at a time.

Other Debt Relief Remedies

Using Your Home's Equity to Consolidate Bills

Many people will use the equity in their home by either refinancing their current loan or taking out an equity line of credit to pay off their bills.

A problem that many people have had with an equity line of credit is that, not only do they pay off their debts, but they also dip into the credit line to purchase big-ticket items. In essence, the line of credit becomes a credit card.

As equity in different areas and communities began to drop, the lenders who were carrying the lines of credit began to freeze the borrower's credit lines. Borrowers were no longer able to tap into their line of credit. Payments and balances were still owed.

Equity lines of credit are more difficult to obtain because of the economic meltdown, but they are doable. The key factor a lender will look at when you apply is your credit report and FICO score, how much equity you have, your monthly income, and job stability. If you do qualify for an equity line of credit, make sure that you are saving money and that you do not run up more debt by making additional purchases from the equity in your home.

Refinancing Your Home

If refinancing your home feels like an option to consolidate your bills, make sure you are saving money and will have a lower monthly mortgage payment after all the bills are paid off. For example, if your current mortgage is $1,800 per month and you have credit card payments totaling $500 per month, that totals $2,300. If your new monthly mortgage totals $1,600, you have saved $700 per month, which includes your $500 savings from your credit cards. You can calculate what your potential payment would be by visiting: *www.financialvictory.com/calculator*.

In most cases, there are closing costs involved with a refinance. Get a Good Faith Estimate from your lender to make sure you understand how much these costs will be. If you are refinancing your home to get a lower interest rate and save money or to consolidate your bills into the refinance, your balance and loan amount will go up to include your closing costs. You must determine if the costs of the loan are worth the savings if you decide to move ahead with a refinance.

There are two things to look for when making your decision. First, review how many years you have remaining on your current loan, and second, determine the cost to do it. After weighing your options, you may opt to look for another strategy to get rid of your debt if it doesn't make sense.

To qualify for a refinance, the lender will evaluate your situation by calculating the ratio of your monthly income to your new payment, plus your debts. If the ratio is between 25 and 38 percent, you will probably qualify for the new loan.

It is not recommended that you refinance or get an equity line of credit if your bills will be paid off within a three-year period. Also, a refinance should only be done if your payment will be less.

A danger to refinancing or an equity line of credit is that, if you pay off your debts, you must be responsible and disciplined not to start using your credit cards, starting the cycle all over again. If you can't break the credit card cycle, and continue refinancing to pay back your debt, it will eventually backfire on you when you run out of equity to qualify for the loan.

Help for Seniors

A reverse mortgage is a loan for seniors that uses a percentage of the home's equity. The senior's property is the security on the loan. A lender only approves a percentage of the equity in the senior's home based on the senior's age. The older the senior is, the more money he or she is eligible for.

The amount available for the senior after the calculations are made (based on the age and equity) can be distributed in different ways: a line of credit to draw from as needed, a lump of cash, or a combination of the line of credit and cash. A monthly payment drawn from the line of available credit can also be given to the senior.

The beauty of the reverse mortgage is, if the senior is a homeowner with equity, he or she can use the money to pay off credit card debt, pay off the mortgage (if there is a balance) and have a cushion with the line of credit for emergencies, repairs, medical needs, or any other necessity he or she may have without ever making a payment.

Pressure is taken off the senior, and the loan only has to be paid back if he or she sells the home or dies. Any equity that remains will go to the senior or his or her heirs.

Reverse Mortgage Misconceptions

In the past, reverse mortgages had a negative implication. Many of the misconceptions of the past are incorrect.

Two of the biggest misconceptions with a reverse mortgage are:

1. After completion of a reverse mortgage, the lender owns the house and will take it. This is incorrect. Title of the property will remain in the senior's name, not with the lender.

2. When the senior dies, the bank will get the house and all the equity. This is false. The heirs of the property can sell the property and receive the remaining equity. If the senior dies, the lender wants to be paid back the outstanding balance on the loan. The heirs can sell or refinance the property to pay the lender back.

If you are a senior, you can calculate what you can qualify for by visiting *rmc.ibisreverse.com.*

Accelerate Your Mortgage Payments

Your mortgage is probably one of the largest monthly payments you have. Most people finance their home for 30 years. You can reduce the life of your mortgage by adding additional money to your house payment each month. If you decide that you want to make extra mortgage payments on your loan, make sure you check the box on your statement or write a note for the lender to apply the extra amount towards your principal.

If you decide to set up bi-weekly payments by making a payment every other week on your mortgage, it will equate to making one extra payment a year. Adding one extra payment or more per year will save hundreds of thousands of dollars for the life of your loan and shorten a 30-year loan to approximately 23 years. For this to work, you must be consistent with the payments. The more money you add to your payment, the more years will drop off.

Visit *www.financialvictory.com/calculator* to calculate your bi-weekly payments and see how much you will save on this program.

If you don't want to make bi-weekly payments, there are still a couple of other ways to do this. One way would be to divide your monthly payment by 12 (months). For example, if your payment was $1,800 per month and you divided the payment by 12, it would total $150. Adding $150 to your payment each month would apply that amount towards your principal, reducing your balance more quickly. You can also just add one extra payment per year, which would have the same effect. Both options will also reduce the amount of years.

Using Your Savings Account

Many people want to know if it is a good idea to use the money in their savings account to pay off their debts.

There is no right or wrong answer. Everybody's situation is different. The problem with draining your savings account to pay off debt is that you now have no reserves. Without some sort of cash reserves, if an emergency arises, you will be tempted to go back and start using your credit cards.

Look at the interest rate you are earning in your savings account. For example, if you are earning interest at a 6 percent interest rate and are paying 20 percent or higher interest on your debt, you are losing money.

The best scenario would be to keep a small amount of money in your savings account for an emergency and use the remainder to pay down your debt. With the money you are saving from the debt you just paid off, you can either put it back into your savings account or apply it to your remaining outstanding balances.

401K Withdrawals

Tapping into your 401K account and withdrawing money to pay off your debts may not be a good idea because you are required to pay it back with monthly payments. In most instances, a portion of your paycheck will be deducted toward paying back the money. You will be charged interest as well. If you decide to go this route, make sure you can afford to have this money withdrawn from your paycheck and not go back to using your credit cards. Many people end up in worse financial shape after tapping into their 401K account if they don't change their old spending habits. You can also be taxed on any money that has been withdrawn.

In some instances, if you have a 401K with your current employer, you may not be able to withdraw unless there is an emergency, such as a medical problem.

Consult your financial advisor to see if there are any consequences or if there is a better option for you. The best advice is not to tamper with your 401K.

Consulting a Credit and/or Debt Management Company

If you are delinquent in your monthly payments, over-extended with your credit cards, see a problem making your future monthly payments, or are tired of paying high interests, you should consider contacting a credit counseling and/or debt management company to consolidate your debt.

A good credit and/or debt management company will review your budget and financial situation to see if you are eligible for their program. Before your initial contact with a credit counselor, be sure you have a list of your bills showing the creditor's names, balances owed, interest rates, and payments due. Also have information regarding your income and living expenses available. Once the counselor has this information, he or she will evaluate your income, assets, debt, and expenses to determine what you can afford to pay each month.

Credit counselors become the middle party in communicating with your creditors. The creditor will take your situation more seriously and be more willing to work with you if you are in a debt management program. The credit counselor will help you work out a repayment program with your creditors.

Tell your credit counselor about any late notices, demand notices for payment, collection notices, legal suits, court judgments, or anything that you feel is significant for the counselor to review. The counselor needs to see the whole picture in order to develop a payment plan that will help you and satisfy the creditors.

Once the counselor receives all the required information from you regarding your financial situation, he or she will contact your creditors to work out a repayment schedule. You will be required to close the accounts that are being repaid through this program.

In structuring a workable program, the credit counselor will work with the creditor to lower your payments by reducing the interest rates. Each creditor will have a different formula used to lower the rate. Some may be as low as zero or as high as 11 percent or more.

A reduction in your interest rate will cause the payments that you were currently paying to be less. With the reduction of the interest rate, the payments will apply more toward your principal, which will allow you to pay off your debts in less time.

By participating in a debt management program, you will save thousands of dollars in interest and be debt-free in a shorter time than you would by doing it yourself. You will be paying off all the accounts that you have enrolled in the program. Late fees and over the limit fees will stop being accrued by working with a credit counseling company. When you are in the program, you will make one monthly payment to the debt management service to cover all your debts. Your payment will then be disbursed to the creditors.

Most reputable credit counseling and/or debt management are nonprofit organizations. A good company will spend more time with you to assess your situation and charge only a nominal monthly fee to be in the program.

There are several good credit counseling companies such as Consumer Credit Counseling Service, but the company we recommend is Cambridge Credit Counseling. You can contact them at: (800)208-5084.

Bankruptcy as a Last Resort

Bankruptcy should be your last resort in resolving your problem. Before ever considering bankruptcy, it is advisable to exercise and exhaust all other options. Consulting a credit counseling or debt management company may be your best solution, especially if you are considering a Chapter 13 repayment plan.

There are circumstances in which filing bankruptcy may be your best solution. It's not the end of the world, but you need to make sure you are doing it for the right reasons, not because you feel like you can't handle the collection and creditor calls.

There are certain steps that you must take when filing for bankruptcy. The first thing you should do is contact an attorney.

An attorney will review your situation and help decide what type of bankruptcy you are eligible for, as well as what is required in your state.

In 2005, bankruptcy laws changed. The new law requires an individual to take a means test to determine if you are eligible for either a Chapter 7 bankruptcy, in which most of your unsecured debt is discharged, or a Chapter 13, in which you are put into a repayment program. This means test requires you provide information of recent income over the last few years, past tax returns, pay stubs, a list of your debt and names of creditors, monthly expenses you incurred, and a list of all your property, which also includes personal property, such as electronics. Another new requirement is that a person seeking bankruptcy relief is required to have counseling by a credit counseling company.

If you are considering filing for bankruptcy, you should always seek the advice of an experienced bankruptcy attorney. Trying to do it yourself can be risky. A bankruptcy attorney can review your situation and determine if you are eligible to file for a Chapter 7 bankruptcy.

A Chapter 7 bankruptcy requires a filing fee to the court. This must be done within six months of completing your credit counseling course. Once you have filed for bankruptcy, you will be assigned a court date and you must attend this initial court date. The creditors that you listed to be discharged in the bankruptcy have the option to attend the court hearing. A trustee will be appointed to oversee the bankruptcy.

The trustee's role is to determine what assets you have that can be sold to pay off your creditors. The trustee will also evaluate and determine what debts you have that are eligible to be discharged through the bankruptcy.

You will no longer owe a debt that is discharged through the bankruptcy. Debts that are dischargeable include most unsecured debts, such as credit cards, medical bills, collection accounts, payday loans, unsecured business debt, judgments, and rent.

Debts not dischargeable through a bankruptcy include most student loans, some overdue taxes, alimony, child support, and fraudulent loans.

A Chapter 13 bankruptcy is known as the federal repayment plan or wage earner's plan. Most people are put into the Chapter 13 program. Many people file a Chapter 13 because they are allowed to keep all their property, including their cars, home, or furniture, while lowering their payments. The court will assign a trustee to determine how much a person should pay per month to settle the debts.

In filing for a Chapter 13, a detailed budget must be filed showing your current living expenses and bills that are owed. A proposed amount that you can pay to each creditor must be submitted to the trustee, who will disburse to the creditors.

Once the court approves your payment proposal, the payments will begin. The court will determine the term you have to pay the debts. At the end of the term, any amount still owed on the debt is forgiven by the court.

You must be employed and earn enough money to meet your budgeted living expenses, plus the payments you agreed to pay by the court trustee to qualify for a Chapter 13.

Whether you file for a Chapter 7 or Chapter 13, you must complete a credit counseling class prior to filing your bankruptcy case.

You will also need to complete a second debtor education class after you file your bankruptcy petition and documents. Once the class is completed, you will need to file a form with the court that indicates that you have completed an approved Debtor Education Class.

Both a Chapter 7 and Chapter 13 will appear on your credit reports for up to 10 years from the discharge date.

As you can see, there are many different ways for you to eliminate your debt. You may find you can combine several suggestions in this chapter. The main thing to remember is that you need to stay focused and disciplined. Reward yourself with something small when you have succeeded in paying off each debt. You're going to make it!

SECTION II:

CREDIT REPAIR 101

7

THE ROLE OF CREDIT REPORTING AGENCIES

Most people do not understand how the credit reporting agencies actually work. In the good ole days, when you were in the market for credit, all you had to do was complete an application and turn it in to the bank. The bank manager would review it and either approve or deny the application.

Things have changed tremendously throughout the years. Credit applications are processed differently and are now dependent on a credit reporting system that only merchants or lenders who are subscribers can access to determine if you are credit worthy.

When you complete any type of application for credit, there is tiny print underneath the signature line authorizing that company to run your credit report for review. It also states that, if you are approved, you also are authorizing them to report your payment history to the credit reporting agencies.

Bingo! That is how you make your entrance into the credit reporting world. If you've ever owned a credit card or applied for a loan, then you have a credit history. Your credit history is compiled and maintained by credit reporting agencies.

There are three major national credit reporting agencies. TransUnion, Equifax, and Experian collect your credit history from creditors that subscribe to their services, such as credit card companies, banks, mortgage companies, and other creditors. They also tabulate a credit score based on your credit activity.

Whenever you apply for credit, the bank or credit card company will request a copy of your credit report from one or more of these credit reporting agencies to review your credit report and credit score. The information on your credit report will determine whether the lender will extend you credit or a loan and what interest rate you qualify for based on your credit history and credit score.

The credit reporting agencies have a lot of power. If a subscriber of the credit reporting agency enters one bad entry on your credit report, you can be affected for many years for future credit. If a person inputting data strikes the wrong key and creates a negative error on your credit report, you will be adversely affected.

According to a study from the Public Interest Research Group, one out of every four credit reports contains serious errors: debts wrongfully listed as delinquent, closed accounts listed as open, debts that belong to other people with the same name, and so on. Human error can harm an individual for many years unless the consumer finds the mistakes and challenges them with the credit reporting agency.

Functions of the Credit Reporting Agencies

The three major credit reporting agencies, TransUnion, Equifax, and Experian, collect and report credit information. Every month, lending institutions and other creditors who are subscribers to the credit reporting agencies will send updated consumer credit information to one or more credit reporting agencies. This information includes how much an individual consumer owes on each of his or her accounts and whether he or she makes payments on time.

Whenever you apply for a credit card or a loan, all of that information is also sent to the credit reporting agencies and is viewed as an inquiry.

The three credit reporting agencies also search public records for financial information, such as court records from bankruptcies, judgments, tax liens, and foreclosures.

There are two types of inquiries: a hard inquiry and soft inquiry. A hard inquiry is one made by institutional creditors, such as credit card companies, store and automobile merchants, mortgage lenders, and rental applications to a landlord. A soft inquiry is made by the consumer him- or herself or by an employer.

Credit reporting agencies only share credit reports and scores when there is a request, authorized by the consumer to the merchant, to receive a copy of their report. No one can randomly get a copy of your credit report unless you authorize it.

Credit Report Entries

Credit entries, whether positive or negative, can remain on your credit report for specific periods of time. Entries remain on a credit report as long as an account is open and active.

Negative entries, such as collection accounts, delinquent accounts, charged off accounts, foreclosures, judgments, and paid tax liens can remain on your credit report for up to seven years from the date of the last activity.

Bankruptcies can remain on a credit report for up to 10 years from the discharge or filing date. Unpaid tax liens do not have a date that they can be removed until they are paid, and then the seven year period will begin.

Inquiries can remain on a credit report for up to two years from the date of the initial inquiry.

Any positive credit that is paid off will remain on the credit report up to seven years from the date it was paid off. Then it drops off.

An important thing to remember is that the dates are reflected on the last date the activity took place, not the reporting date. For example, if you had an account that was put into collection on 4/2/09 and the last activity with the original merchant was 3/1/07, the last activity date is 3/1/07. That means it will be removed from the credit report seven years after the last activity date (3/1/07).

The three major credit reporting agencies are independent companies that each collect information in different ways and possibly from different subscribers. Therefore, a credit report from Experian may have different information than a credit report from TransUnion, and may also differ from Equifax. Again, it may be because not every creditor and lending institution will report to all three credit bureaus because that leads to discrepancies.

Who Sees Your Credit Report

Anytime you sign a document indicating you give permission to have a credit report run to view your history, the company or individual you submit it to has that right.

Credit reports are often requested by employers or future employers, landlords, and insurance companies. If you own your own business, some of the potential vendors with whom you are seeking a business relationship may pull your credit history.

In some cases, employment can be denied, and, believe it or not, insurance companies can deny your coverage or penalize you with higher premiums for having a poor credit rating. Housing can be an issue with a landlord if he or she feels you are a risk after reviewing your report. That's why it's so important to make sure that everything on your credit report is true and accurate.

Laws to Help the Consumer

In 1971, the Fair Credit Reporting Act (FCRA) was enacted. With new and recent legislation, it states that United States citizens have the right to receive free access to their credit reports and credit scores from each of the three national credit reporting agencies. If an application is denied, the consumer is eligible for a free credit report from the credit reporting agency from which the vendor requested information. The vendor requesting the credit report must send you a letter within 30 days of the denial naming the credit reporting agency or agencies if more than one was used. If you were not denied credit, you can still order your credit report for a fee if you have already received your free annual credit report.

This act also forces the credit reporting agencies to list any inquiries that were made on the credit report. With this law, you are allowed to dispute inaccurate, erroneous, and incomplete information being reported. The credit reporting agency must respond within 30 days of receiving your dispute and allow you to put a statement or comment on your credit report stating your side of the story.

Another act that protects the consumer with regard to his or her credit report is the Fair and Accurate Credit Transactions Act of 2003 (FACTA). This act gives the consumer the right to request one free copy of his or her credit report from each of the major credit reporting agencies every year. FACTA also includes several provisions protecting the consumer against identity theft.

To request a free copy of your annual credit report, the following options are available. You can request either one or all three reports.

Phone : (877) 322-8228

Website: *www.annualcreditreport.com*

Mail: Annual Credit Report Request Service

P.O. Box 105281

Atlanta, GA 30348-5281

When you request a copy of your credit report, you will need to include your personal information, such as name, birth date, Social Security number, and current address.

If you are requesting your credit report from the Website, you will be asked questions that must be answered correctly regarding your accounts. Once you have completed the information and answered all the questions correctly, you will be able to download your credit report.

When requesting a credit report by mail, you will not only need to provide your name, birth date, Social Security number, and current address, but also two other forms of identification, such as a utility bill, driver's license, bank or credit union statement, government-issued ID, and so on. This must match your current address.

Proof of your Social Security number is also required, which could be a copy of your Social Security card, a letter from the Social Security Administration, a military ID, or a Medicaid or Medicare card.

Your birth date must be proven as well, which would be from your driver's license, birth certificate, passport, or government-issued ID.

With so much identity theft, the credit agencies want to make sure you are who you say you are.

Your free annual credit report does not include your credit score, which can be purchased separately.

Remember, if you are requesting your credit report and you are married, you both have separate reports, which must be requested separately.

8

UNDERSTANDING YOUR CREDIT REPORT

Most people have problems understanding what their credit report is saying about them. It is important that you request a copy of your credit report at least once a year, or more often if you are trying to make a large purchase, such as a home or automobile. You need to make sure there are no problems or errors on your credit report before a lender or creditor reviews it.

As mentioned in the previous chapter, you can receive one free copy of your credit report annually by requesting it at: *www.annualcreditreport.com* or if you have been denied credit. If you have already received your annual credit report, you still can order it for a fee. You can request it individually from each of the credit reporting agencies. Every state has a different fee, so call or visit them online to make your request and find out what the fee is, as well as their address if you choose to mail your request.

TransUnion: (800) 888-4213 *www.tuc.com*

Equifax: (800) 685-1111 *www.equifax.com*

Experian: (888) 397-3742 *www.experian.com*

Refer to the previous chapter for the items you will need to request your credit report, such as name, address, Social Security number, and birth date, as well as two additional forms of identification.

Once you have received a copy of your credit report from all three of the credit reporting agencies, review each entry. Each of the credit reports has a breakdown of their codes to help you understand the report.

Breaking It Down

A credit report is basically divided into four sections: identifying information, credit history, public records, and inquiries. When you get your credit report, you need to review every section to make sure it is accurate.

Section One: Identifying Information

In this first section, it is important that you review each entry. Don't take it for granted that everything is correct. This section will include:

- ✓ Name
- ✓ Current address
- ✓ Social Security number
- ✓ Date of birth
- ✓ Spouse's name (if applicable)

Other information may include your previous addresses, telephone numbers, driver's license numbers, and your employer.

Section Two: Credit Summary

The credit summary section of your credit report will summarize information about the different types of accounts you have. This section lists the total number of accounts you have, the total of all your balances, and the number of current and delinquent accounts. It will include the following account types:

- ✓ Real estate accounts, including any mortgages that you have.
- ✓ Revolving accounts, such as credit cards and lines of credit.
- ✓ Installment accounts, such as loans.
- ✓ Collection accounts.

Your credit summary will also summarize the number of accounts you have open and closed, number of public records, and the number of inquiries made against your credit within the past two years.

Section Three: Account History

The account history section of your credit report contains the bulk of the information. It sometimes is referred to as tradelines. In this section, each of your credit accounts and the details of how you have paid or are currently paying is listed. Each account will include the name of the creditor and the account number. Sometimes the account number is scrambled or may be shortened for security purposes.

Each listed account will contain several pieces of information, including:

- ✓ **Company Name.** The company reporting the information.
- ✓ **Account Number.** Your account number with the company.
- ✓ **Responsible Party.** The primary person responsible for the account and the type of participation you have with the account. Abbreviations may vary depending on the reporting agency, but here are some of the most common:

- ❏ I - Individual
- ❏ U - Undesignated
- ❏ J - Joint
- ❏ A - Authorized User
- ❏ M - Maker
- ❏ T - Terminated
- ❏ C - Co-maker/Co-signer
- ❏ S - Shared

- ✓ **Date Opened.** The month and year you opened the account with the credit grantor or company that has issued you credit.

- ✓ **Months Reviewed.** The number of months the account history has been reported.

- ✓ **Last Activity:** The date of the last activity on the account. This usually is the date of your last payment.

- ✓ **High Credit.** The highest amount charged or the credit limit that you were approved for. If the account is an installment loan, the original loan amount will be listed.

- ✓ **Terms.** For installment loans, the number of installments or the amount of the monthly payments may be listed. If this is a revolving account, this column is usually left blank because there is no ending date.

- ✓ **Balance.** The amount you owed on the account at the time it was reported. Even if the account is paid off every month, a balance can still appear that was not posted at the time of reporting.

- ✓ **Past Due.** Any amount that has past due payments at the time the information was reported.

- ✓ **Status.** A combination of letters and numbers are often used to indicate the type of account and the payment history, such as being current or past due.

Abbreviations for these types of account are as follows:

- ❑ O - Open
- ❑ R - Revolving
- ❑ I - Installment

Numbers are used to represent how current you are in your payments. For example, a current account or paid as agreed would be shown as 0 or 1. The numbers can vary from 0 up to 9. Any number larger than a 1 will cause your credit report to reflect negative information, causing your credit score to go down.

For example, an I2 rating would mean an installment loan you have is 60 days late.

Another example would be an R9 rating which means the revolving account is in collection or has been charged off.

Charged off means the creditor has given up on you and after many efforts to collect the debt, they eventually write it off. In many instances, the account usually is turned over to a collection agency.

- ✓ **Date Reported.** The last time information on this account was updated by your creditor. Some report monthly, some report quarterly. Every creditor is different on the dates they report credit activity.
- ✓ **Collection Accounts.** Collection accounts may appear as part of the account history or in a separate section. Where it appears depends on the company providing your credit report.

If you've had any accounts referred to a collection agency within the last seven years, this section is where the account will be reported. The name of the collection agency will be listed along with the amount owed, the name of the original creditor, last activity date, and contact information.

Section Four: Public Records

The public records section lists public record items that were filed with the county recorder. These may include liens or claims from local, state, and federal courts with regard to your history of meeting your financial obligations. These include:

- ✓ Bankruptcy records.
- ✓ Tax liens.
- ✓ Judgments.
- ✓ Foreclosures/Notice of default.
- ✓ Child support (in some states).

It doesn't list arrests or criminal activities, just finance-related data. These are the entries that will really hurt your credit faster than anything else.

The entry will list the type of filing, such as a tax lien or bankruptcy. It also has the filing date, the status of the entry, the liability amount, a docket number (reference number), closing date (when it was paid or satisfied), and the county in which the recording took place.

Credit Inquiries Section

There is a credit inquiry section in the credit report that lists the parties who have accessed your credit report within the past two years. When you get a copy of your credit report, your version of the credit report will list all of the credit inquiries that have been made. Not all of these inquiries will appear on the lenders' and creditors' versions. Only "hard" inquiries are shown to lenders. These are inquiries made when a lender checks your credit report to approve your credit application.

Your version will also include the "soft" inquiries that were made by your existing lenders and creditors and other lenders who want to solicit you for promotional purposes. The soft inquiries are not counted in your credit score.

Additional Information Section

This section consists primarily of former addresses and past employers as reported by your creditors. Review this section for accuracy.

Warnings About Credit Report Requests

✓ **Never order your credit report from an advertisement on television, radio, or the Internet offering a free credit report.** These are merchants that will cause a "hard" inquiry on your report, which can lower your credit score. Only order your credit report directly from the main reporting agencies. If you order yours directly, there is no inquiry listed that will hurt your credit score.

✓ **Beware of imposter credit reporting sites.** There are Websites that contain domain names similar to annualcreditreport.com. They take advantage of common misspellings that are close to the word that you misspelled. Some of these sites ask for highly sensitive information such as names, Social Security numbers, and addresses to steal a consumer's identity and apply for credit in his or her name. To avoid these scams, you might consider ordering your free annual credit report by phone, not online.

✓ **Check your kids' credit reports.** It is unbelievable, but identity thieves are increasingly targeting the personal information of kids under 18 years of age, who are required by law to have a Social Security number before their first birthday. Parents can safeguard their children against such fraud by checking their child's credit report annually with all three of the major credit reporting agencies. By requesting the credit report, you are looking to see if there is a credit report associated with your child's social security number and identification. There shouldn't be any activity, or credit card or bank accounts opened, unless the child did it.

Keep Yourself Informed

As you continue to monitor and review your credit report, you will be able to be informed on what is going on with your credit. A credit report with errors on it will cause you problems when you are trying to make any type of purchase.

Once you have a copy of your credit report, you will be able to repair whatever inaccuracies are being reported on it. When your credit report is where it should be and is reporting accurate information, your credit score should increase to help you qualify for whatever credit you are applying for.

9

THE CREDIT REPAIR PROCESS

You've done your preliminary legwork in trying to get your finances back in order by making your financial goals, setting up your budget, finding ways to save money, and requesting a copy of your credit report.

Now that you have a copy of your credit report from all three of the credit reporting agencies, its time to roll up your sleeves and tackle the inaccurate information that is being reported on your credit report.

Jim and Tammy's Story

Jim and Tammy came to our office to have their finances reviewed. The past couple of years were rough on them because Jim had been laid off from his job. They tried to keep up with their bills using their savings and Tammy's income. After several months, Jim was back to work and it was catch-up time.

As we reviewed their current financial situation, we were able to help them come up with a budget and plan to pay everything off. It took them some time to pay their debts off, but with hard work and sacrifice, they succeeded.

With their problems behind them, they felt that they were back on their feet and able to purchase a home. When they went to the lender to be pre-qualified for a mortgage, they were shocked to find out that their credit scores had dropped so low that they were not eligible for a loan.

They came back to our office to discuss their situation. Because they were turned down for their loan, we told them that they qualified to receive a free credit report. Because all three credit reporting agencies were used to get their scores, they requested all three.

When they received their credit reports, they discovered several accounts that were inaccurate. Some of the balances that they paid off were still showing as owed and other entries were reporting delinquencies that they knew were wrong.

As we reviewed each of the items, we showed them what they could do by disputing the inaccuracies with the credit reporting agencies. It took many months to do this, but they were able to eliminate the inaccurate items by having them corrected or removed altogether. With the improvement on their credit reports, they were able to turn their situation around and qualify for a home of their dreams.

The first mistake Jim and Tammy made before coming back to us for help was not requesting a copy of their credit report from all three credit reporting agencies prior to pre-qualifying for a loan. If they had done this first, they would have discovered the errors and tried to correct them before submitting an application.

Reviewing Your Credit Report

As you review each of your credit reports, whether it be on the credit reporting agency's Website where you can download it, or a hard copy of your report that you received in the mail, it is important that each of the entries are being reported accurately.

If you find information on the credit report that is inaccurate or incorrect, the Fair Credit Reporting Act states that you have the right to dispute the entry with the credit reporting agency. The credit reporting agency must reinvestigate the entry with the creditor. The investigation must be completed within 30 days of receiving your letter of dispute.

If the creditor doesn't respond within that time period, the credit reporting agency must remove the entry you are disputing from the credit report. If the creditor does respond and corrects the inaccurate entry, the credit reporting agency will update your credit report. There is also the possibility that the creditor may respond and not make any changes to the credit report. If you are not satisfied with your updated credit report, you can write a 100-word statement on any of the remaining items on the credit report explaining your side of the story. This consumer statement will then appear on your credit report every time it is run. If you don't want to write a 100-word statement on your credit report, you can write another dispute letter 120 days from your most recently updated credit report.

The Disputing Process

The first thing you need to know is that you must dispute your inaccurate information with all three credit reporting agencies separately. The disputed entry may or may not be on all three credit reports. Remember, subscribers may not subscribe to all of the credit reporting agencies. That is why you will see that some of the creditors on one report are not on the others.

Even if all three of the credit reporting agencies have the same information, it does not mean that if an item comes off of one credit report that it will come off the others. There is no guarantee what the outcome will be. That is why you must dispute any inaccurate information on each separate report.

When disputing with the credit reporting agencies, you can use their dispute forms, write your own letter, or dispute the item online at their Website. If you decide to dispute through letter-writing, just state the facts in a simple and concise sentence or two.

If you are viewing your credit report on the credit reporting agency's Website, there will be an opportunity to dispute the inaccurate entries online. The site will have boxes to check off next to an appropriate reason for the inaccuracy. You can also use the same responses that are applicable if you choose to write a personalized letter. Sample responses would be:

- ✓ This is not my account.
- ✓ This was not late as indicated.
- ✓ This was not charged off.
- ✓ This was paid off in full as agreed.
- ✓ This was not a collection account.
- ✓ This is not my bankruptcy as indicated.
- ✓ This is not my tax lien as indicated.
- ✓ This is not my judgment as indicated.

If you have found more than four entries that you need to dispute on your credit report, don't dispute everything in one letter. Whether you write a letter, complete their form, or respond via the Website, break your disputes up. Either mail or go back into the credit reporting agency's Website every 30 days and dispute up to four more items. Don't exceed that amount. If you have less than four items to dispute, go ahead and dispute the remaining entries. Continue the 30-day spacing between disputes.

After each letter is sent, expect to receive an updated credit report approximately 45 days after you mail your letter or dispute online. If you haven't received your updated credit report before it's time to dispute the second time, go ahead and mail your second letter or dispute online anyway.

Once all your dispute letters are mailed or uploaded on their Website, and all the updated credit reports are received, review what items were removed or corrected. If you need to do the process again for the remaining items, space the next round of disputes 120 days from your most recent update.

Don't:

✓ Alter or try to change your identity.
✓ Make up a fictitious story.
✓ Dispute any information that is 100 percent accurate.

Do:

✓ Handwrite your letters if you decide to mail them. If a letter looks professional, the credit reporting agencies may suspect that a credit repair company has prepared it, and they will not investigate the dispute.
✓ Use a letterhead (if you have one) with your handwritten letter.
✓ Use the dispute form that the credit reporting agency includes with your credit report if you want to.

✓ Include any documentation showing that the inaccurate entry is incorrect.
✓ Include the identification number listed on the credit report on all correspondence.

Common Credit Report Errors

Remember, each of the three credit reports may have different errors. It is not unusual to have an account reported positively on one report, but negatively on another report.

Here are some of the most common credit report errors.

✓ Wrong, name, addresses, or phone numbers listed.
✓ Information belonging to someone else with the same name.
✓ Duplicate information on the same account, whether positive or negative.
✓ Accounts have negative information that should be positive.
✓ Balances on accounts that are paid off are still showing.
✓ Accounts reporting delinquent that were never paid late.
✓ Incorrect credit limits are shown.
✓ Accounts included in a bankruptcy showing still owed.
✓ Incorrect dates of activity.
✓ Past-due payments that are not owed.
✓ Court records, such as judgments and bankruptcy, that are wrongly associated with you.
✓ Tax liens that are not yours.
✓ Foreclosures that never happened.

Spotting Possible Identity Theft

Reviewing your credit report could also spot possible identity theft. That is why you should request a copy of your credit report at least once a year or every six months.

Things to look for would be:

- ✓ Account names and numbers you don't recognize.
- ✓ Loan applications you don't remember filling out.
- ✓ Addresses where you haven't lived.
- ✓ Soft inquiries by employers or landlords you don't recognize.

Creditors Can Help

Many times, if you have had an account with a creditor for a long period of time, you can contact them directly and explain the error that is being reported on your credit report.

Ask them to write you a letter with the correction and mail to you. Also ask them to contact each of the credit reporting agencies that is reporting this incorrect entry to make the correction.

Once you get a copy of the letter from the creditor, make a copy of it and attach the letter to the dispute letter you are sending. Mail it to the credit reporting agency and ask them to update their files. Once this is done, the credit reporting agency will send you back an updated credit report.

Credit Rescoring

Rapid rescoring is an expedited way to correct discrepancies on a consumer's credit file. The bad news is that you cannot do this yourself. A rapid rescore dispute process works through lenders and mortgage brokers, a handful of authorized credit reporting repository companies, and the credit reporting agencies.

If you are a borrower who is eligible for a rescore on your credit report, you would be required to provide specific documentation that would be sent to the credit repositories working on your file. The credit repository is the company that the credit grantors use. The credit repository receives its information from the three major credit reporting agencies and must verify the initial information provided by the consumer for a rescore. Once the verification is input into the repository's system, a new score is generated.

The main thing to remember is that a rapid rescore may only be temporary. You may be able to close a loan with it, but you must follow through with the three main credit reporting companies in making sure it was removed or corrected on your credit report. If it reappears, submit the documentation to the credit reporting agencies directly.

The benefit of a rapid rescore is that you save time from having to dispute directly with a credit reporting agency that may take more than 30 days to complete an investigation. If the closing of a home or mortgage is dependent on your credit score and you are in a time crunch, the rapid rescore is your best solution.

100-Word Statement

The Fair Credit Reporting Act states that you can add a 100-word statement to your credit report on entries that you feel you should address.

Is it a good idea? It all depends on what you are hoping to accomplish. If it is just airing out your frustration and it makes you feel better, go ahead.

Will it make a difference on how a potential creditor will view your credit report? Probably not! Most of the time, a creditor is not going to take the time to read your statement. The credit grantor is primarily looking for two things: your credit activity and credit scores.

If you decide to add a 100-word statement to your credit report, have it removed before you make any attempts to dispute the item.

If you leave it on your report and try to dispute it separately, there is a good chance the credit reporting agency will consider it frivolous and will not honor your dispute.

Use caution when adding a statement to your credit report. It may come back to bite you.

Example Credit Report Dispute Letter #1

May 10, 2011

Regarding Identification #: 11111111

Dear Customer Service,

My name is Sam L. Jones. I am responding to a credit report I received from your company. After reviewing the report, I have found errors listed on it. They are as follows:

This account at Neddy's Department store, account # 12340, was never paid 30 days late. Please correct this.

My account at Main Bank was paid off in full and not charged off. This needs to be removed from my credit report. Please remove this.

I do not owe this tax lien, docket #333333.

I never had an account with Consumer collection account # 1212121. This is not mine.

My current address is 14311 Maple Ave., Anytown, CA 99999. My Social Security number is 111-22-0000. My previous address was 78765 Taft Park Way, Anytown, CA 99999. My birth date is 12/7/70.

Sincerely,

Sam L. Jones

Example Dispute Letter #2

[NOTICE THE DATE IS 30 DAYS LATER]

June 10, 2011

Regarding Identification #: 1111111

Dear Customer Service,

My name is Sam L. Jones. After a careful review of my credit report, I have discovered errors. They are as follows:

This Bankruptcy docket #875621 for $135,000, dated 10-21-2008 is wrong and should not be on my credit report. Please remove this.

My account at Mays Jewelers, account number 43258 was paid off in full and not a collection account. Please remove this.

Auto Mart Corp., account number 6324571 was paid as agreed and should have a positive rating. Please correct this.

My current address is 14311 Maple Ave., Anytown, CA 99999. My Social Security number is 111-22-0000. My previous address was 78765 Taft Park Way, Anytown, CA 99999. My birth date is 12/7/70.

Sincerely,

Sam L. Jones

Should You Use a Credit Repair Company?

Using the services of a credit repair company is basically hiring a company to do what you can do yourself. There really are no secrets to the process. All the credit repair company is doing is disputing information with the credit reporting agencies about negative entries on your credit report. Many companies will indicate they have relationships with the credit reporting agencies or they have a secret way of getting the creditors to remove the negative entries. This is more than likely not true because the credit reporting agencies are regulated under the Fair Credit Reporting Act both by state and federal laws.

When you contract with a credit repair company, you will be charged a fee. Some services will pull your credit reports or request you get your own reports. The letter-writing campaign will begin after you have contracted with the company.

The reasons some people will hire an outside credit repair company is that they feel intimidated or don't have the time to do the work themselves. There are many safeguards that you must take before signing up with a credit repair service. Many companies are operating illegally and you don't want to be caught in that trap.

Beware of Credit Repair Scams

Unfortunately, when people are desperate and going through financial challenges, it is easy for them to fall prey to credit repair scams. If you are searching for a credit repair company, here is how to tell if it is a legitimate or scam company. Some scam companies may sign you up for their services only to take your money and run. Here is a list of things that should raise a red flag.

✓ The company wants you to pay for credit repair services before it provides any services. Under the Credit

Service Organizations Act, credit repair companies cannot require you to pay until they have completed the services they have promised.

✓ The company doesn't tell you your rights and that you can do this for yourself for free. This should be listed in any contract it provides you.

✓ The company recommends that you do not contact any of the three major national credit reporting companies directly. It knows if you do that you may discover it took your money and is doing nothing.

✓ The company tells you it can get rid of all the negative credit information in your credit report, even if that information is accurate. Nobody can guarantee any one item for improvement on your credit report.

✓ The company suggests that you try to create a "new" credit identity. This is called file segregation. It is done by applying for an Employer Identification Number to use instead of your Social Security number to create a new credit report. This is totally illegal.

✓ The company advises you to dispute all the information in your credit report, regardless of its accuracy or timeliness. If the information is 100 percent correct, you have no grounds for a dispute.

Remember, if you are given illegal advice and follow it knowing it is illegal, you may be committing fraud, and will find yourself in legal hot water.

It's against the law and a federal crime to lie on a loan or credit application, to misrepresent your Social Security number, and to obtain an Employer Identification Number from the Internal Revenue Service under false pretenses. You could be charged and prosecuted for mail or wire fraud if you use the mail, telephone, or Internet to apply for credit and provide false information. Most applications that you sign have a statement explaining that by signing the application, the information you provide is true.

The Credit Service Organizations Act

Credit repair services are regulated by the Credit Service Organizations Act under state and federal law. Under this act, most states require credit repair companies to be registered and bonded in each state where they do business. Each state has different requirements. You should review a copy of the Credit Service Organizations Act for your state before signing up for this service. The Federal Trade Commission and State Attorney General's offices are going after credit repair companies that are not compliant with the laws and are soliciting business with misleading information. You can also get a copy of the federal version of the Credit Service Organizations Act by visiting: *www.ftc.gov.*

Some of the main declarations of this law are for the protection of the consumer when signing up with a credit repair company. A credit repair company must give you a written contract that spells out your rights and obligations approved by its state. Be sure to read these documents before you sign anything. And before signing, know that a credit repair company cannot:

- ✓ Make false claims about its services.
- ✓ Charge you until it has completed the promised services.
- ✓ Perform any services until it has your signature on a written contract and has completed a three-day waiting period. During this time, you can cancel the contract without paying any fees.

Before you sign a contract, be sure it specifies:

- ❑ The payment terms for services, including the total cost.
- ❑ A detailed description of the services the company will perform.
- ❑ How long it will take to achieve the result.
- ❑ Any guarantees the company offers.

- ✓ The company's name and business address.
- ✓ Name and address of the surety bond company, if applicable.

What Should You Do?

Everyone's situation is different. If you feel you can do your own credit repair yourself, do it. If you decide to hire a company, you can save money by going to a company that provides you a total service by counseling and reviewing your budget, debt, and credit report, as well as provides tools to repair your credit, get on track with your budget, and get out of debt. Contact Professional Credit Counselors at: *www.financialvictory.com.*

Check any company you are considering with the Better Business Bureau.

Have You Been Victimized?

If you feel you have been victimized by a credit repair scam, state law enforcement officials may be helpful if you've lost money. Laws are in place to protect you. You can contact your local consumer affairs office or your state Attorney General (AG). Many AGs have toll-free consumer hotlines; check your telephone directory for the phone number or *www.naag.org* for a list of state attorneys general.

10

IMPROVING YOUR FICO CREDIT SCORE

FICO credit scores are top secret. The secret is not the actual score itself, but how the score was calculated. FICO Scores are calculated from different entries of data that has been entered in your credit report. This data can be grouped into five categories:

- ✓ Payment History: 35% of your score
- ✓ Amounts Owed: 30% of your score
- ✓ Length of Credit History: 15% of your score
- ✓ New Credit: 10% of your score
- ✓ Types of Credit You Use: 10% of your score

A credit score, also known as a FICO score, is a three-digit number determined from your credit reports. The three major credit reporting agencies have a slightly different formula for calculating their scores and will reflect different numbers. Equifax's score is called BEACON, TransUnion's is called FICO Risk Score, and Experian's is called FICO II. FICO scores range from 300 to 850.

When lenders review your application, they use the scores from the credit reporting agencies to determine a borrower's potential risk of paying back the loan. The higher the score, the more likely a borrower will be to repay the loan.

There are five major categories that comprise your credit score. Review each category and its importance to your overall score.

Five Major Scoring Categories

Payment History: 35% of Your Score

Your payment history is one of the biggest factors when it comes to your score. The payment history evaluated would be on specific types of accounts that you have, which would include credit cards, retail accounts, installment loans, finance company accounts, mortgages, and so on.

Items that adversely affect your credit score would include public records such as bankruptcy, judgments, lawsuits, tax liens, foreclosures, collection items, and/or accounts that are delinquent.

Other contributing factors include:

- ✓ Severity of delinquency.
- ✓ The amount that is past due on delinquent accounts or collection items.
- ✓ Time lapse since past-due items or public records.
- ✓ Number of past-due items on file.
- ✓ Number of accounts paid as agreed.

Amounts Owed: 30% of Your Score.

Any outstanding balance that is owed on credit cards, car loans, mortgages, and other types of accounts will be reflected in this percentage of your score. Someone who is overextended on his or her debts will be penalized. Being overextended may lead to late payments, or eventually no payments at all. This factor determines if you can currently manage more credit responsibly.

One of the biggest causes of a lower score is when the proportions of the balance to the original credit limit is too high. Other contributing factors include:

- ✓ Amount owed on specific types of accounts.
- ✓ Number of accounts with balances.
- ✓ Proportion of credit lines used.
- ✓ Proportion of installment loan amounts still owing.

Length of Credit History: 15% of Your Score

The older your credit history is, the more it will increase your score. Other contributing factors include:

- ✓ Time since accounts opened.
- ✓ Time since accounts opened, by specific type of account (installment or revolving credit).
- ✓ Time since account activity.

New Credit: 10% of Your Score.

If you open several new accounts, or have several inquiries on your credit history in a short period of time, it can reduce your credit score and will affect your chances of qualifying for credit. Contributing factors include:

- ✓ Number of recently opened accounts.
- ✓ Proportion of accounts and types of accounts that are recently opened.
- ✓ Number of recent credit inquiries.
- ✓ Reestablishment of positive credit history following past payment problems.

Types of Credit You Use: 10% of Your Score

Credit mix, meanwhile, is somewhat of a vague category, but repaying a variety of debt indicates the borrower can handle all sorts of credit. The type of credit use doesn't usually play a big role in the lender's decision in extending you credit. It could make a difference if you do not have a lot of information in the other factors. If that is the case, this factor will become more important.

The type of mix with your credit, such as credit cards, loans, finance accounts, and mortgages you have will also play a role. You may carry a variety of credit cards, but for your credit score, there are really just two types: retail cards, which include stores and gas cards, and bank credit cards. Bank cards such as Visa and Master-Card will increase your score slightly. Retail or merchant cards still give you points, but the bank cards are the best.

A FICO score takes into consideration all these categories of information, not just one or two. Your FICO score is only derived from the information from your credit report. The important thing that is evaluated is the mix of information in your credit report, which varies from person to person.

FICO Credit Scoring Risk Factors

- ✓ Below 585: Very High Risk. May not qualify for loan or credit.
- ✓ 585–619: High Risk. May not qualify for the best rates.
- ✓ 620–679: Lender may take a closer look at credit report.
- ✓ 680–718: Good Credit.
- ✓ Above 719: Excellent Credit.

What's Not Included in Your Credit Score

FICO scores are tabulated by the activity of the five categories previously mentioned. In reviewing your own personal credit report, you can see there is other information listed pertaining to your history. However, it is not considered a part of your credit score. Information that does not count would be:

- ✓ Race, color, religion, national origin, sex, and marital status.
- ✓ Age.
- ✓ Income, occupation, title, employer, date employed, or employment history.
- ✓ Where you live.
- ✓ Interest rates being charged on credit cards or other accounts.
- ✓ Child/family support obligations.
- ✓ Consumer-initiated inquiries that you initiated yourself.
- ✓ Promotional inquiries that were made by lenders in order to pre-screen you for a pre-approved credit card offer.
- ✓ Administrative inquiries that were made by lenders to review your current accounts with them.
- ✓ Whether or not you are participating in a credit counseling of any kind.

Ways to Increase Your FICO Score

There are several ways to increase your FICO scores. It is not a speedy, overnight happening, but with a plan and a strategy, you can do it. When you implement your plan, you may have to wait to see the results.

Every month, semi-monthly or quarterly, the credit grantors will report updated information to the credit reporting agencies. Make sure you check your credit report to determine how often your credit grantors are reporting your activity. It is only when they report to the credit reporting agencies that you will see changes and new activity on your credit report.

Here are some ways for you to increase your credit score. Don't forget to check all three credit reporting agencies and request your score once you have had a change in your status with the creditors.

- ✓ Pay your bills on time.
- ✓ Look for errors on your credit report and have them corrected.
- ✓ If you have missed payments, bring the accounts current. The longer you pay your bills on time, the better your credit score.
- ✓ If you are having trouble making ends meet, contact your creditors or see a legitimate credit counselor. This won't improve your credit score immediately, but if you can begin to manage your credit and pay on time, your score will get better in time.
- ✓ Keep balances below 30 percent of your credit limit on credit cards and other revolving credit.
- ✓ Don't close unused credit cards. Closing unused accounts without paying down your debt changes your utilization ratio, which is the amount of your total debt divided by your total available credit. It can lower your credit score.
- ✓ Don't open a number of new credit cards that you don't need.
- ✓ If you close any accounts, leave the oldest ones open.
- ✓ Transfer balances from a card that's close to being maxed out to other cards to even out your usage.
- ✓ Use multiple cards to charge and keep balances low.

You don't want to put too high a balance on one card. Spread it out. For example, try to get the cards you are using to 20 to 30 percent of your credit limit instead of having several cards with a zero balance and others with balances of 80 percent of the credit limit.

Vantage Score

As if it wasn't confusing enough learning about FICO scores, the three national credit reporting agencies (Equifax, Experian, and TransUnion) are also involved in a joint venture to produce a credit score for businesses and consumers called the Vantage Score.

The Vantage Score is expected to compete with the FICO scores. FICO scores have been the most dominant in the credit scoring industry.

The Vantage Score will have a score range between 501 and 990. The higher the score, the more creditworthy the applicant appears. As with the FICO score, the higher a score is, its assumption is that the applicant will have a lower risk of defaulting with his or her credit obligations.

The Vantage Score will use the same scoring criteria for each of the three national credit reporting agencies. If your credit data in one bureau is different from the other credit bureaus, there still will be a difference in your credit score from one agency to the next.

Vantage Scores differ somewhat from FICO scores, because they use both a letter grade (A–F, like a report card) and the numeric scale ranging from 501 to 990.

What Determines Your Vantage Score?

According to Vantage Score, LLC. the breakout of your Vantage score is as follows.

Payment History	How timely and consistent your payments are.	32%
Credit Utilization	How much credit is available and the debt (balances) to credit limit ratios total.	23%
Credit Balances	Total of your outstanding balances.	15%
Depth of Credit	Credit types and length of credit history.	13%
Recent Credit	Recent accounts opened and total of recent hard inquiries.	10%
Available Credit	The total dollar amount of credit that you could potentially utilize.	7%

Credit Score Confusion

FICO and Vantage Score use two different numerical ranges. As previously mentioned, the FICO scale runs from 300 to 850, while the Vantage Score begins at 501 and runs to 990. The credit reporting agencies say the Vantage Score range is more "intuitive," because it breaks down like an elementary school report card. Here is a look at how they rate you.

- ✓ 901–990 = "A" credit
- ✓ 801–900 = "B" credit
- ✓ 701–800 = "C" credit
- ✓ 601–700 = "D" credit
- ✓ 501–600 = "F" credit

To receive a copy of your Vantage Score, visit: *www.experian. com/consumer-products/vantage-score.html*

SECTION III:

A FRESH START

11

REBUILDING AND REESTABLISHING YOUR CREDIT

After coming out of a financial crisis that damages your credit and causes you such mental stress, you'll probably feel so beaten down that you never want to have another credit card or loan. Sounds like a good idea, but living in today's society you need to have a credit card to rent a hotel or car, and credit established to purchase a home.

You don't have to be in debt to have credit. That is where you need to change your way of thinking. Look at any new credit that you reestablish only as a way to rebuild your credit portfolio, not to get into debt again. The question is, how do you go about reestablishing and building new credit with a tarnished credit report? There are ways for you to accomplish this. Having a strong credit report is your goal. Repairing and restoring your credit report is the main thing, but there are other things you must do.

Open a Personal Secured Loan

Open up a personal secured loan at your bank with a savings or CD account that will earn interest. Find out what the bank's minimum deposit requirements are and what you can afford. If there are no minimum deposit requirements, make a $300 to $2,000 deposit.

When you have deposited the money, ask the bank for a loan against the money in your account. The money in your savings or CD account is what will be used to secure the loan. The bank does not have any risk if you do not pay the loan back because the money in your account is their security if you default on the loan. During the time of the loan, you cannot draw money out of it.

Each bank has its own requirements and generally will not allow you 100 percent of your deposit. The bank may determine you can borrow only 80 to 90 percent of the amount you have in your account. A repayment agreement will be drawn up with the bank. Many banks will set up the terms of the loan, including a monthly payment and a date for the loan to be paid back. In some instances, your bank may only ask for one payment (known as a balloon payment) to be paid back at the end of the loan period.

If monthly payments are required, make sure your payments are paid on time and that the bank reports this to the credit reporting agencies to establish a good payment pattern.

If you open another account with other banks, repeat the same process. This would show more than one good account being reported on your credit report.

Merchants

Merchants are another great way to establish new credit. Jewelry stores, furniture stores, tire shops, and appliance stores all offer credit. Before applying with any of these merchants, explain your current situation and your past problems on your credit report. Many times these merchants will set up a credit line for you that will be reported on your credit report. If they are reluctant, offer to pay the account off in 90 days. If they agree to it, be sure you make the payment on time, and that they are subscribers to the credit reporting agencies. If the merchant is not a subscriber to a major reporting agency, don't make the purchase. You only want a merchant that is a subscriber and can report a good payment pattern to the credit reporting agency.

Repeat this procedure at least two times with other merchants to get more positive entries on your credit report.

Secured Credit Cards

A secured credit card is a great way to reestablish credit. Secured credit cards do not look any different from a regular Visa or MasterCard.

To qualify for a secured credit card, a consumer must open a savings account with a bank that offers secured credit card programs. A deposit must be made, which the bank will specify. The deposit can range from $300 to $5,000. Each bank sets the amount required. The bank, in return, will issue the customer a Visa or MasterCard securing it with the full amount of the deposit, or a percentage of the amount deposited. For example, if you deposit $300, your credit limit is $300; or, if you deposit $1,000, and the bank you deposited with will allow you to charge up to 50 percent of your deposit, it would be $500.

The banks that offer the secured credit card programs will pay interest on your deposit; however, they will also charge interest on the use of your card with the purchases you make. Some banks may also charge a yearly annual fee for a card.

A one-time processing fee may be charged by the bank with the initial application. An annual fee will be charged once the application is approved. The annual fee will be charged directly on your credit card once a year.

Before opening up an account, make sure you understand the terms of the card.

Questions to Ask

✓   What is the annual fee?
✓   How much is required to deposit?
✓   How much of the deposit can be used to charge?
✓   What is the interest rate for the deposit?
✓   How much interest is charged for purchases made with the credit card?
✓   When does the interest charge begin?

If you decide to get a secured credit card, the payments you are making on the credit card will be reported on your credit report.

To make sure that the credit card activity is being reported monthly, charge a small amount each month and pay it off each month. For example, charge $25 each month and pay it back in full when the payment is due. The purpose of the secured credit card is not to run up debt, but to establish a good payment pattern. If you do keep a balance on the card, make sure it is 30 percent below your credit limit to improve your FICO score.

Once you have established a good payment history for at least 12 to 24 months with the bank you have the secured credit card with, find out if you can get an unsecured credit card for which no deposit is needed.

If you do not get a secured credit card through your bank, there are other banks that have these types of programs. Most of the banks offering the secured programs will be out of state. For a list of banks offering an unsecured credit card, visit: *www. bankrate.com.*

If you decide to go with an out-of-state bank, be sure to mail your deposit by registered mail, with a return receipt. *Do not give your money to anyone besides the bank!*

A word of caution: When reading advertisements for a secured credit card, make sure the name of the bank that is offering the program is in the ad or the application. Call the bank directly to make sure they really exist before submitting the application. Check the Better Business Bureau and Internet to make sure it is not a scam company.

Co-Signer

If you do not want to get a secured credit card to establish or reestablish your credit, you can ask a friend or relative to co-sign with you for a loan or credit card. This is risky for the person co-signing. In most instances, you may need a co-signer for a secured type of loan, such as a car or mortgage.

A co-signer is a person who completes an application for credit with you and is responsible for the debt if you fail to pay back the money. A co-signer must qualify for the line of credit, and sign papers stating that he or she will be responsible for the payment if you default.

The account that is opened for you with a co-signer who has guaranteed the loan is usually reported to the credit reporting bureaus in both names. Payments will be reported on your credit report as well as the co-signer's report. If the payments are made when due, there is no problem because your rating will be good, but if they fall delinquent, it will reflect on both you and the co-signer's credit report.

Once you get reestablished with your own credit history, refinance the loan you have with the co-signer in your name only and remove his or her name. For example, if you have a co-signer for a car, after your credit history has improved, refinance the car with the bank or loan company to remove the co-signer from the loan. The same would be true with a credit card or mortgage.

Friend or Relative

A friend or relative can help you establish credit by requesting a credit card in your name from a credit card company they have established credit with. You would be added on for a "user card."

The friend or relative can apply for a new credit card or add your name onto the one they already have. The primary person (the friend or relative) would be the one responsible for making the payments on the account.

When approaching this type of situation of asking a friend or relative to add your name to his or her credit card or request a new credit card adding your name, tell this person to keep the card. Your intention is not to use the card, but only to be able to show a good payment history on your credit report as a user.

The key here is that your friend or relative makes timely payments. If he or she falls behind in making any of the credit card payments, both you and the primary card holder will get negative marks on your credit reports.

Once you have established your own credit history, ask your friend or relative to remove your name and cancel your card. This will have no reflection on your credit report.

Automobile

There are dealers who specialize in individuals who have had a bankruptcy or bad credit. Do a search on the Internet as well as your telephone directory. Sometimes you can find car dealers who specialize in these types of problems through their advertisements.

Be prepared to pay a large deposit, and high interest rate. The automobile is the collateral for the loan, and many dealers are interested in helping you.

If you find a car dealership that can work with you, before you sign any contracts, make sure they report your payment history to the credit reporting agencies. Believe it or not, there are some companies that still don't subscribe to the credit reporting agencies. If that is the case, don't buy your car from them. Make sure you work with a company that does report your credit activity. The most important thing is that you make your payments on time to build up your credit report.

Open a Checking and Savings Account

Opening a checking and savings account may not give you credit, but it will help you with the qualifying process for new credit. The lenders like to see that you have money set aside in your accounts.

Mortgage

Depending on the severity of your financial situation and credit rating, some mortgage companies will grant a mortgage to an individual, but they will require a large down payment and charge high interest rates and closing costs.

Before you look for a new home, have a lender pre-qualify you to make sure you can get the loan. Be open and honest about your past so they can get you the best possible loan.

Lenders change their criteria periodically. Always contact a bank or mortgage broker to find out what programs may work for your situation.

Work With Previous Creditors

Contact creditors whose accounts you have paid off in the past to help you reestablish new credit. They may consider it if they see that you were making your regular payments on time before your problems arose, as well as how long it took to resolve those problems.

Debtors Anonymous

A word of caution! Make sure that the financial crisis you are coming out of has ended. You may not be ready to enter the world of credit again. Overspending can be just as hard to overcome as gambling or excessive drinking. Some people are hooked on credit card spending.

There is Debtors Anonymous, a support program similar to Alcoholics Anonymous. They have programs nationwide. Even if you are not hooked on spending, it may be worth your time to get information on this program. Visit their Website at: *www.debtorsanonymous.org*.

You Can Do It!

You are probably wondering how you can get a positive history of your paying habits when you lost everything. Reestablishing your credit will take some time. It is not an overnight process, but it can be done. Be patient and persistent.

12

LIFE AFTER FORECLOSURE, SHORT-SALE, OR BANKRUPTCY

If your financial crisis resulted in losing your home to foreclosure, filing for bankruptcy, or having to sell your home on a short-sale, you're not alone. Having to make the horrendous decision to take those drastic actions probably affected you more than you think. Individuals going through such turmoil are often left depressed and uncertain about their future and feel as though it's the end of the world. You may even wonder if life can ever be the same. The good news is that once you pick yourself up and regroup, you will be okay. Learn from your mistakes, but take this opportunity to get a fresh start. That's what this book is about, and what we tell our clients to do. The pain will ease as you develop a plan on how to rebuild your life.

Don't let bankruptcy or a foreclosure define who you are. Consider it a very large bump in the road, but not one that will stop you from rebuilding your life.

The truth is that most foreclosure, short-sale, and bankruptcy victims will eventually be able to get new credit and/or purchase a house in the future. It is not the end of the world. It just is going to take some work.

There are things you need to do to regroup and correct your situation so that when you are ready to buy a home or apply for new credit, you are in a position to do it. You don't want a replay of your past situation. You need to have a solid plan for the future, and the time to start is now. The amount of effort you put in will determine how long it will take for you to rebuild your finances, your credit, and your life.

Coping with the emotional stress of this situation is sometimes more difficult than the financial aspect. Knowing your options before, during, and after foreclosure can help you make better decisions. Remember these three things:

1. **Always keep your perspective.** Don't allow your mind to keep going back to the negative things that have happened. Keep your focus on the end result of your new, fresh start.

2. **Create a positive plan.** Having a plan in place will help you succeed in your financial goals. Refer back to Chapter 1 to create your plan of action. By having a positive plan, you can refer to it and chart your successes.

3. **How you survive a foreclosure, bankruptcy, or short-sale is up to you.** You can walk around with your head down, or you can hold your head up with confidence that you are going to conquer this new financial endeavor.

A New Attitude Toward Debt Is Necessary!

✓ Everything we use credit for can be obtained without it. Analyze what you can afford and define whether the purchase is a "need" or a "want."

Managing debt properly requires doing without some of the things you want. That means paying cash or waiting until you can save for it. Sometimes it requires sacrifice on your part, but it will eliminate an impulse purchase.

✓ Keep a daily expense journal. This one exercise will help you manage your money by writing everything down you spend money on daily. Sometimes it is a rude awakening of how much money is being wasted on trivial things.

✓ Cut back on purchases that are not necessary, or lessen the amount of times you get that mocha or latte.

✓ Switch from brand names to generic names, clip coupons, and look at the sale items. Become a frugal shopper.

There are different things you can do to build yourself up emotionally, mentally, and strategically. Here are some steps to help move you forward.

Step One: Create a Spending Plan

Create a spending plan to focus on your immediate financial obligations. Remember to always pay your basic needs: food, medical bills, housing expenses, utility payments, car loans, child support, and income tax debts.

If you are currently in a financial crisis and need help, apply for social service programs that can provide emergency housing and utility vouchers and/or food to assist you during this transition.

Step Two: Set Financial Goals

Now is the time to ask yourself what your top financial challenges are and how you are going to overcome them. Take a look at what your top assets are. Things to look at would be:

- ✓ Available cash or equity.
- ✓ Job potential.
- ✓ Ways to increase your income.
- ✓ Envision what your life will be in one to five years down the line. This will help you set your goals and work toward them.
- ✓ Decide to focus attention on saving, reducing debt, and increasing your income.

Step Three: Estimate Next Year's Income and Expenses

Before you can estimate next year's income and expenses, you need to review your past year's spending to see what possible changes can be made.

Because your lifestyle has changed and you have probably downsized your housing and living expenses, you will probably be able to manage your money better.

Things to do would be:

- ✓ Review current debts and expenses.
- ✓ Consider how your expenses will change given your new housing situation.
- ✓ Determine if the new housing situation will have any impact on other costs, such as gas, traveling to and from work, and day care.
- ✓ Fine-tune expenses and create a livable spending plan.

Step Four: Analyze Your Spending Habits

Your past spending habits may need to be changed for your future. It becomes a family affair that everyone needs to be involved with.

- ✓ Review the balance and payments of each debt. List changes you would like to make with your debt. This becomes your action plan.
- ✓ Review monthly expenses with family members. Rank your expenses from most to least important.
- ✓ Find ways to start saving money. Every little bit helps. Start saving $10 or more a week and put it an interest-bearing account.

Step Five: Create a Rebuilding Plan

Your plan for rebuilding your finances can be accomplished in many ways. This includes:

- ✓ After your new spending plan has been implemented, tackle the negatives on your credit history.
- ✓ Begin establishing new credit and a good payment history.
- ✓ The new plan should support paying all monthly bills on time.
- ✓ Pay off past-due balances or bring them current.
- ✓ Create a written plan that is clear and attainable. Don't make your plan unrealistic. Take baby steps.
- ✓ Start an emergency fund. Make sure you have at least three to six months' worth of living expenses put aside.
- ✓ Start putting together a financial plan for your retirement, or perhaps a college plan for your children if you are raising a family.
- ✓ Make sure you have adequate life insurance to protect your loved ones.

✓ Open a savings account and start putting aside at least 10 percent of your income every month. If you do this consistently, in a few years, you can have enough money to use for a down payment on your next house.

Step Six: Changing Habits

Change is hard to do. A habit is created when you do the same thing over and over. Trying to break old money habits that don't benefit you is hard, but repetition of doing the right thing will make it come easier. Remember:

✓ Resisting change and clinging to old habits will not move you forward. Financial freedom is a choice you make with each spending decision based on your new savings goal.

✓ Pay off debt rather than incurring new debt.

✓ Don't rob Peter to pay Paul. In other words, don't use one credit card to make payments on another card.

✓ Determine your monthly bill-paying habits, such as record-keeping, periodic reviews, and tracking expenditures.

✓ Keep track of your checking account balances and reconcile monthly.

Step Seven: Managing the Plan

Managing your finances and the plan you have implemented is important in this process.

✓ Keep your savings goals in a visible place to review often.

✓ Have someone keep you accountable. This could be a spouse, relative, or outside credit coach or counselor.

✓ Don't get discouraged—even one step at a time will still achieve progress.

✓ Have a bookkeeping and tracking system in place, such as Mint (free personal finance software at *www.mint.com*), Quicken (*http://quicken.intuit.com*), or an expense journal, and balance your checkbook regularly.

Finding a New Home

Try not to worry about being able to find a new home. There are some things that you can do to prepare yourself when the time comes to relocate.

It may take you several years before you can purchase a home, but you definitely need a roof over your head.

Applying for a house or an apartment to rent before the foreclosure or bankruptcy hits your credit report will of course benefit you; however, the timing might make it hard to do that.

If your credit report becomes an issue in renting another place, stay positive and be determined not to give up. With so many people in similar situations, landlords may look for other things.

Large apartment complexes have strict approval criteria and will pull credit. Instead, look for a rental in a townhouse, condo, apartment, or home that is owned by a single landlord. These types of landlords are less likely to do credit checks.

When talking to the landlord, ask what criteria is used to approve tenants for the rental. If a credit check isn't one of them, then you have less to worry about.

Whether you are able to get around the credit check or you get approved for an apartment or home despite your credit history, expect to pay more money up front.

You need to set money aside for your move and be in a position to offer to pay a larger deposit. Another option would be to offer to pay a higher amount of rent, or pre-pay several months in advance on the rent.

Hitting a Brick Wall

If you are having a hard time and continue to get rejections, there are other alternatives.

- ✓ Get someone to vouch for your financial responsibility, such as previous landlords, your bank, or current or previous employers.
- ✓ If you have past-due accounts, pay them off and get the creditor/lender to write a letter stating the account has been paid in full.
- ✓ Write your own letter explaining your situation and what caused your financial problem. If you have supporting documents, show them as well.
- ✓ Use a co-signer.

Creative Financing to Buy a House

If you have been able to save money for your move, and don't want to rent, you still can buy a house, but there are only a few ways to do this.

Owner Financing

You may be able to find a home for which the owner is willing to carry the financing. Some owners will help a buyer by becoming the bank. In other words, if you purchased a home for $200,000 and had $20,000 to use as a down payment, the seller may offer to finance the $180,000 instead of you going to a bank to get a new loan. Both you and the seller would agree to the terms, such as the interest rate that you would pay, the payment, and the length of time for the loan.

If the owner is comfortable after reviewing your situation, job stability, and income, a note will be drawn up for you to make payments to the owner. Be prepared to give a down payment toward the sale price.

Most owners finance for less time than a bank, but that gives you time to get back on your feet and refinance the loan in the future, which would pay off the owner.

Lease Purchase or Option to Buy

Another alternative may be to look for an owner who will allow you to lease the property with an agreement that within so many years, you will purchase it.

An option fee would be required such as 3 to 5 percent of your agreed price to purchase. The monthly payments you would make would go towards the purchase price. The lease purchase or option to buy would have a date that the sale must be completed. The sale price is locked in, so when you exercise the option to buy, the sale price doesn't change. Most lease purchases or option to buy agreements can run from one to four years. It is all negotiable.

Have a Family Member or Friend Buy the House.

If you have a family member or friend who agrees to purchase the house that you want to buy, the loan would be solely in that person's name. It probably would be financed as an investment property because he or she would not be living in the property. You will be the one making the payments.

Once the loan is completed, your family member or friend can add you onto the title of the house and have it recorded. By having your name listed on the title, when you are in a position to refinance the property, it will be easier for you to do. When you do refinance, you can put the property in your name.

Housing Guidelines for Foreclosures, Short-Sales, and Bankruptcies

Most loans must conform to Fannie Mae and Freddie Mac guidelines with lenders making conventional-type loans. Fannie Mae and/or Freddie Mac purchase loans from the banks and lenders. They have set certain guidelines for the lenders to make the loan package saleable. This is another way a lender or bank makes money.

Fannie Mae or Freddie Mac can change their guidelines on what they will accept or approve at any time. The current guidelines pertaining to individuals who have suffered a foreclosure, short-sale, or bankruptcy to qualify for a conventional Fannie Mae or Freddie Mac loan are as follows:

Derogatory Event	Waiting Period Requirements	Waiting Period Extenuating Circumstances
Bankruptcy:		
Chapter 7 or 11	4 years	2 years
Chapter 13	2 years from discharge	2 years from discharge
Foreclosure	7 years	3 years with additional requirements
Deed-in-lieu/ short-sale/ pre-foreclosure	2 to 4 years, depending on down payment	None

Extenuating circumstances are nonrecurring events that are beyond the borrower's control, which result in a sudden, significant, and prolonged reduction in income, or a catastrophic increase in financial obligations.

If a borrower claims that derogatory information on their credit report is the result of extenuating circumstances, the lender must substantiate and document it. Examples of documentation that can be used to support extenuating circumstances include:

✓ Documents that confirm the event, such as a copy of a divorce decree, medical reports or bills, notice of job layoff, job severance papers, etc.

✓ Documents that illustrate factors that contributed to the borrower's inability to resolve the problems that resulted from the event, such as a copy of insurance papers or claim settlements, property listing agreements, lease agreements, tax returns covering the periods prior to, during, and after a loss of employment, etc.

The lender must obtain a letter from the borrower explaining the documentation. The letter must support the extenuating circumstances and confirm the nature of the event that led to the bankruptcy or foreclosure-related action, and illustrate that the borrower had no reasonable options other than to default on his or her financial obligations.

It is important that when you are in the market to purchase a home and you have had any of these events take place that you contact a mortgage broker or bank to see if the guidelines have changed.

FHA Guidelines

FHA also has set guidelines for qualifying for a home loan. Their guidelines are not as strict as Fannie Mae or Freddie Mac for a future purchase. FHA's guidelines can change also, so it is important that you follow up with the bank or a mortgage company to get the most recent guidelines. FHA guidelines for the following are:

Chapter 7 Bankruptcies

✓ A borrower is eligible for financing 24 months after the discharge date and must have reestablished good credit history.

✓ A borrower whose bankruptcy has been discharged for less than 12 months is not eligible.

✓ If a mortgage was included in the Chapter 7 bankruptcy, it would be considered a foreclosure, unless the mortgage was reaffirmed.

✓ Credit must be reestablished. If three traditional lines are not available, two lines of traditional credit must be open for at least 12 months, and 1 non-traditional line must be open for four to seven years with no late payments in the last 24 months (excludes medical collections). There can be no late payments since the bankruptcy.

Chapter 13 Bankruptcies

Chapter 13 bankruptcies are allowed to enter into the mortgage transaction after 12 months of the payout period, provided performance has been satisfactory and the borrower receives court approval. It must be a refinance and is a cash-out situation that allows the bankruptcy to be paid off in its entirety.

Short-Sale or Foreclosure

A short-sale is treated just like a foreclosure. There must be at least 36 months from the date the redemption period ends and the property officially goes back to the bank.

Your Mental Health Is Important

Having financial issues can destroy your marriage, family, relationships, and self-esteem. Divorce often accompanies financial loss. Shame can be a very powerful, negative force. Do not let this overcome you. It is important that you seek out resources to help you on a personal level through your church, synagogue, therapist, and supportive friends. Here are some added things to do.

✓ **Exercise.** Research has proven that exercise is great for stress relief (even a 10-minute walk).

✓ **Take care of yourself.** Take time for yourself and get extra rest.

✓ **Spirituality.** Embrace spirituality in the way you feel comfortable and that is positive to you.

✓ **Seek professional help** anytime you feel the need.

✓ **Communicate.** Talk to your friends or spouse about your thoughts.

✓ **Write.** Putting things in writing can give them new meaning. Read what you have written. Make a list of positive things in your life.

✓ **Organize.** Get organized and stay organized. Once you establish a system, either online or with folders, continue to follow it.

Whatever your circumstances were, remember that they are no longer of any consequence, unless you allow them to be. Pick yourself up and quit blaming yourself or others for what has happened. The past is behind you, but your future is an unlimited, boundless opportunity to succeed.

13

QUALIFYING FOR CREDIT

Obtaining credit is an art. Many times when people complete a credit application, they don't realize the liability and seriousness of what they are signing. An application for credit can become a legal document that, if not completed accurately or contains misrepresentations, can be used against you if there is ever a court action on the credit you were approved for.

Who Qualifies for Credit?

Creditors are looking for potential applicants for credit cards who are 18 years old or older. There are certain requirements that must be met to get approval of a credit card. Listed are various age groups who will qualify for credit.

High School Students

Believe it or not, a high school student who is 18 years of age may receive an application to apply for a credit card. In most cases, an 18-year-old is a senior in high school or a recent graduate.

This type of application will probably only be approved if a parent guarantees payment for the credit card. This is probably not a good idea.

The important thing to be aware of is that many of the applications for credit for a young adult or student will require a co-signer. Some companies will issue credit cards to a young adult without a co-signer, providing he or she is a full-time student. The credit limit would be minimal.

College Students

College students may apply for credit cards. Many credit card companies would give full-time students credit. The procedures are similar to the high school student's application as previously discussed. In the application, it is necessary to indicate the name of the college or university and submit some type of proof of attendance. This can be done with a college or university statement, or a report card. The credit limit would be minimal. A co-signer is not usually required.

Employed Individuals

An individual who has been employed for a minimum of one to two years has a good chance of qualifying for a line of credit or credit card. Frequently on the credit application, there will be an amount stated for qualifying. For example it may say, "Applicant must make $12,000 gross income per year to apply." This must be verifiable to the creditor should its agents decide to call or write your employer.

The higher the income, the higher the line of credit that will be granted. The creditor is looking for stability. Besides being stably employed, the credit grantor will look at the credit report history, credit score, and length of residence. All factors are taken into consideration to determine credit eligibility.

Unemployed Individuals

Creditors are looking for job stability. If an individual is unemployed, it is best not to apply for a line of credit or credit card. The risk of repayment is too high and the application more than likely will be denied.

If an individual has been employed, but has been laid off the job and is not working, the credit that has already been established will not be affected, providing the accounts do not become delinquent. If the accounts become delinquent, the creditor may close the account.

If a creditor feels a high risk of not receiving their payments, they may cancel the account. Frequently, if the situation appears to be temporary, creditors will probably work out a repayment plan.

Self-Employed Individuals

Self-employed individuals have a harder time qualifying for credit than someone who is employed by an employer. When a creditor looks at an application from a self-employed individual, the individual must have been self-employed for a minimum of two years. The best way to show the creditor that the risk is minimal is to provide two years' tax returns, or a 1099 form (if you are an independent contractor) with the credit application. This is verification to the creditor of your business income.

An independent contractor is someone who is labeled self-employed. It may be in real estate sales, consulting, car sales, insurance, or the like. At the end of the year, anyone who is paid by commission will receive a 1099 form naming the company he or she worked with, and the amount of commissions received. This 1099 form should be photocopied and returned with the credit application.

After the applicant submits the necessary verifications of income, the creditor will review the applicant's credit report, and other pertinent factors. If the credit score is high enough and the creditor feels secure with the application, the line of credit will be approved.

As you can see, it is important to do your homework before applying for credit. You want to make sure that you are approved the first time and that your application is complete.

All credit grantors have their own form of processing and evaluations, so if one turns your application down, you still may be able to qualify with another company.

Qualifying for Credit

Most of the time, people never read the fine print that authorizes a credit grantor to review their credit report and to verify the information they have completed on the application, such as employment and bank accounts.

Learning what the potential credit grantor looks for prior to filling out your application can help you avoid a credit denial.

Credit vs. Debt

You can have credit without having debt. Not all credit is bad, but some people think that just because they have credit cards and lines of credit that they must use them. Credit cards or lines of credit should only be used for an emergency, convenience, and building your credit history.

With that being said, whatever the reason you are using the credit card, you must be sure that you pay the balance off in full each month. If you can't pay it off in full, set a goal to have it paid off within a few months and don't charge anything else until you do.

The only good credit to have with outstanding balances would be for purchases that you are building equity in, such as real estate investments.

The Three Big "C"s of Credit

Before you apply for any type of credit, whether it is for a credit card, a mortgage or a loan, there are several things credit grantors are looking for. The main thing they want to see is your ability to repay the debt.

Creditors are looking for the three big "C"s of credit: capacity, character, and collateral. Once you understand the importance of the three big "C"s, you will feel more confident when you turn an application in.

Capacity

The creditors' main concern is how you are going to pay the debt you are applying for. When you are completing your credit application, notice the amount of questions pertaining to your employment, how long you have been employed, the type of work you do, and of course, your salary and any bonuses you may receive.

The creditor will review the monthly expenses you have listed, as well as compare them to what your credit report lists. They also want to know how many dependents you have, and if you are paying child support or alimony.

Once these factors are determined from your application, your debt-to-income ratio will be calculated. In most cases, a bank or lender will not lend you money if the ratio is more than 50 percent. Before you apply for credit, find out what the ratios are for that company. (Complete the Debt to Income Calculation Worksheet.)

Debt-to-Income Calculation

Gross Monthly Income

Salary $_____

Spouse's Salary $_____

Commissions $_____

Bonuses $_____

Alimony $_____

Child Support $_____

Other $_____

Monthly Fixed Expenses

Rent/mortgage $_____

Automobile $_____

Automobile $_____

Bank installments $_____

Charge/
Revolving Accts: $_____

Child Support: $_____

Alimony $_____

Other $_____

Total income: $_____
(before taxes)

Total expenses: $_____

Proposed
loan payment: $_____

Total payments: $_____

The total monthly payments _____ divided by the total monthly gross income _____ equals your debt ratio_____.

Character

Creditors will look at your credit history and your paying habits from one or all three of the credit reporting agencies. Another thing they are looking for is the length of time you have lived at your current address, and whether you own or rent your home. If you have moved several times within the past two years, they will ask for your previous addresses. They are looking for stability.

Collateral

The creditor is looking at what assets you have, such as a savings account, investments, or real estate and property you own. These assets can be liquidated if you fall on financial difficulties. If you show these assets, the credit grantor will look at this as security for the loan.

Creditors want to know they are protected if you stop paying on the loan or line of credit. Having assets in addition to your income from your job can put the creditors' minds at ease.

It is important that you excel in all three areas. This will increase your chances of an approval. You need to know where your strengths and weaknesses are before you apply for credit. Answer these questions before you complete an application to see your strengths and weaknesses.

- ✓ How long have you been employed with your current job?
- ✓ How long have you been in the same line of work?
- ✓ Are you self-employed?
- ✓ How much is your income?
- ✓ Are you paid on commission only?
- ✓ Do you have credit now?
- ✓ Are you aware of any problems on your credit report?
- ✓ Have you paid your monthly obligations satisfactorily?
- ✓ Do you own or rent your home?

✓ How many years have you lived at your current
address?
✓ Do you have a checking and/or savings account?
✓ What debts do you owe at the present time?

Credit Criteria

The following criteria are reviewed carefully by the credit grantors before they will approve a loan application. It is broken into different segments.

Employment

✓ How long have you been employed with your current job?
✓ How long have you been in the same line of work?
✓ Are you self-employed?
✓ How much is your income?
✓ Are you paid on commission only?

These are questions that will provide answers for your character and capacity to repay the loan or establish credit. If you have been employed for less than one year, or show irregular employment, the application will be rejected. If your income is irregular or unstable, your application will also be rejected.

Previous Credit

✓ Do you have credit now?
✓ Have you established credit in the past?
✓ Have you paid your monthly obligations satisfactorily?

Credit grantors will look at your past payment patterns by obtaining a copy of your credit report. They will be able to see what obligations you presently have, and if the accounts were satisfactorily paid. Most credit grantors will assume if you paid your past obligations on time, you will continue the same pattern. If you were negligent and irresponsible with your past credit, you would probably follow the same pattern. Problems can occur to prevent you from making your payments. Occasionally an explanation of the problems and how they were corrected is all a credit grantor needs to know to approve an application. If your credit history is poor and unclear, you will be rejected. Work on repairing and restoring your credit report.

Current Residence

Do you own or rent your home? If you own your home, lenders will feel more at ease with the application. They know that there is more stability. It would be hard to run away if there was a problem. Also, there may be equity built up in your home if you ever needed to sell it or draw money out of it.

If you are renting, then the credit grantor will look at how long you have been at the residence. They also will want to know how long you were at your previous address. The key is once again stability. If your residence is one year or less, there is a high chance of rejection.

Checking and Savings Account

Do you have a checking or savings account? Creditors want to know that you have money in a checking account to write checks and cover your payments. Having a savings account is an extra bonus. You are showing you are able to save money that can be used for emergencies.

Open Accounts

What debts do you owe at the present time? If you are current on all your outstanding accounts, this shows the credit grantor that you are responsible. It also shows your ability to pay.

A Complete and Accurate Application

All information you complete on your credit application will be compared with your credit report. Creditors will reject an applicant if there is information not included in the initial application that appears on a credit report.

Be sure that all the information on the credit application is verifiable and correct. If you give information that is not correct or falsified in any way, the credit application will be rejected. If the creditor did approve the application and found out later that the information given on the credit application had fraudulent intent, they could come back and sue you.

Reasons for a Credit Denial

There are several reasons that a credit application can be rejected. They are as follows:

- ✓ **No credit history.** This pertains to a person who has never had an installment type of loan that would appear on a credit report. When a credit report is run on an individual, and there is no payment pattern or history, or FICO credit scores, the credit report will come back as "No Record Found." This is almost as severe as having bad credit, because a credit grantor cannot distinguish a payment pattern or credit score and will deny the application.

- ✓ **Negative or derogatory credit.** When a credit report is run on an individual, the report has codes that will rate the items on the report. It indicates positive or negative information. The negative items that show up can be charge-offs, slow payments, delinquent accounts, repossessions, judgments, tax liens, and so on.

- ✓ **Low FICO credit scores.** Having too low of a credit score can disqualify you from the type of credit you are applying for. This is also matched up with your credit report activity.

✓ **Excessive inquiries.** Anytime you apply for credit, the creditor will run a credit report. It is then reported on any subsequent reports that an inquiry was made on a particular date by XYZ company. If you were turned down for the credit, the next creditor will more than likely turn you down, too. Excessive inquiries within a six-month period will hurt your chances of getting credit. Five inquiries with denials will probably cause the application to be rejected.

If the creditor does consider approving you for the credit, it may require a letter of explanation for the inquiries. It will also want to know if you were approved and if an account was opened that is not currently showing up.

Remember, if you request a copy of your credit report directly from a credit reporting agency, no inquiry will appear.

✓ **Over-extended.** When a creditor evaluates your application, they take into consideration your monthly income and your monthly expenses. If you are over-extended, or have excessive debt, they may deny your application. Refer back to the debt-to-income ratio worksheet.

✓ **Self-employed.** Creditors feel people who are self-employed have a greater risk factor than those who are employed with others. A person must be self-employed for approximately two years when applying for a mortgage or credit. Each creditor has its own guidelines, so find out what they are prior to applying for the credit.

✓ **Public notices.** A public notice is something that has been recorded with the county recorder. Examples of this are: bankruptcy, judgments, tax liens, notice of default, and foreclosure.

✓ **Additional reasons for a credit denial:**

❑ Insufficient income.

❑ Too short a period of employment.

❑ Sufficient credit obligations.

❑ Failure to pay previous obligations as agreed.

❑ Garnishment, attachment, judgment, foreclosure, repossession.

❑ Bankruptcy.

❑ Insufficient income for amount requested.

❑ No previous bank-borrowing experience within the last 18 months, excluding mortgage.

❑ Unable to verify income.

❑ Unable to verify employment.

❑ Credit application incomplete.

❑ We do not grant credit on the terms and conditions you request.

❑ Present bank references established for less than six months.

❑ Foreigners without permanent resident status (no green card).

❑ P.O. Box as mailing address.

❑ Unlisted telephone number.

❑ No checking or savings account.

Any time there is a denial of credit, the creditor must notify the applicant in writing. The denial letter must include the reason for the denial and indicate which credit bureau was used in reaching this decision. You may request a credit report free from the agency listed, provided the request is made within 60 days of the denial letter (see Chapter 7).

14

THE HOME LOAN PROCESS

More than likely, you are eager to begin your search for a new home. You have waited a long time to restore your credit and put the past behind you. As you know, purchasing a house is probably one of the largest investments you will ever make. You need to make sure you are ready to take the leap and that your finances are back on track.

If you had a past foreclosure, bankruptcy, or short-sale, you need to refer back to Chapter 12 for the guidelines for the type of loan you may be qualified for. Contact a mortgage lender to see if the guidelines have changed and to be pre-qualified for the type of loan that best fits your circumstances. You can visit *www.legacymoney.com* to be prequalified and referred to a lender in your area.

Common Types of Loans

There are different types of loans available for purchases and refinances. When you go to a bank or mortgage lender to qualify for a home loan, they will be able to assess your situation and help you determine the best type of loan for you.

Refinancing Your Home

If you are in the market to refinance your home, you will go through the same process as a purchase. The only difference is that you don't need a down payment and your closing costs can be added into your new loan amount. With a refinance, you can take cash out of the loan if there is enough equity and you are approved.

If you are looking to do a refinance, it only makes sense if your interest rate and payments will be lowered. Sometimes people refinance their homes to pay off their credit card debts. If you are able to pay off your debts within a three-year period, a refinance may not be your best solution. You need to consider how much your closing costs will be because your loan balance will go up. Contact Professional Credit Counselors, Inc. to do a mortgage analysis and access your situation at *www.financialvictory.com*.

Conventional Loans

There are different types of conventional loans a consumer can pick from. They are not government loans, and are primarily made by banks and other such financial institutions. Fannie Mae (FNMA) and Freddie Mac (FHLMC) can purchase these loans on a wholesale basis. There are two variations of conventional loans: conforming and non-conforming. They are based on how high the allowable loan limits are for each county. Your lender will be able to tell you what the lending limits are for your area. Any loans greater than the conforming limit are called non-conforming loans, or Jumbo loans.

Periodically, FNMA and FHLMC will increase or decrease the maximum loan amounts.

- ✓ **A fixed-rate loan** is the most popular type of loan. The interest rate remains the same and never changes.

- ✓ **An adjustable rate loan (ARM)** begins at a lower interest rate. The advantage of this type of loan is that the payment is lower in the beginning of the loan term. Depending on how the promissory note is set up, it can adjust every six months, once a year, or after so many years of being fixed. The rate of adjustment is based on the Index plus the Margin.

  The Index is a rate that is recognized by financial markets, such as: Treasury Bills, Libor Rate, Federal Reserve Cost of Funds Index, Certificate of Deposit, the Prime Rate, etc.

  The Margin is determined by the lender or the investor and becomes part of the promissory note. It can be from a 0 basis point to 2 to 3 points or higher.

  To determine what the interest rate will be after an adjustment, add the Index plus the Margin together. For example, if the Index is 4.50 and the Margin is 2, the interest rate would be 6 1/2 percent.

- ✓ **The Community Home Buyer Program** is available in some communities. This is conventional financing. Some flexibility is allowed for credit problems and lower incomes. This loan has a fixed interest rate and requires a 3 percent down payment. Contact a lender to see if this program is available in your community and if there is any change in the down payment requirement.

Government Loans

✓ **FHA loans** are government-backed loans and very popular for borrowers with low down payments, or who have had credit challenges in the past. There are several different types of loans through FHA. The majority of FHA loans are fixed interest rates, but they also offer adjustable interest rates.

FHA loans can be offered for purchases or refinancing your primary home. They do not finance non-owner occupied investment properties. Contact a lender to see if the rules have changed for refinancing non-owner occupied investment properties.

✓ **VA loans** (known as Veteran loans) are government-backed. You must have served in the military to qualify. The advantage of a VA loan is that no down payment is required. Their qualifications are not as strict for the veteran.

A VA loan is assumable if the veteran sells his or her home. If a buyer purchases a veteran's home and the current VA loan is paid off, the veteran is eligible to get another VA loan.

✓ **Reverse mortgage.** A reverse mortgage is good for individuals over the age of 62. This type of loan is good for a senior who does not owe anything on his or her home or has a low balance on the current loan. The key is the amount of equity in the property. The older the senior is, the more money he or she is eligible for.

Most of these loans are government-backed by HUD and are known as a Home Equity Conversion Mortgage (HECM). This type of loan requires counseling with the senior by a government-approved, nonprofit credit counseling organization.

This loan can have a fixed interest rate or an adjustable interest rate. It allows the senior to pull out a lump sum, create a line of credit, or it can pay the senior a certain amount of money each month.

The beauty of this loan is that there are no monthly payments required. The senior has title of the property, not the bank. If the senior dies or sells the house, the bank will get paid back on what is owed on the balance, and the senior or his or her heirs will receive the remaining equity.

As you can see, one size does not fit all when it comes to selecting a loan type that is best for you. By doing your homework before you begin to look for a new home, or refinance your current home, you will get a better feel of what all your options are to make the right decision.

Remember Your Credit Report and Rescoring

Many people, when deciding to purchase or refinance a home, have no idea what a lender or mortgage company will look for to qualify for the loan.

It is important you know what your credit reports have to say about you for three reasons. The first reason is that the lender reviewing your application will match up what items are on your credit report to your application. If you try to hide any open accounts, you will be found out. Know what items are on each credit report.

The second reason is, if you have had problems in the past with credit, it is best to tell the lender in advance about the situation so it will be able to deal with the problem. Lack of communication will cause denials on loan applications. Occasionally, a letter of explanation may be all that is required regarding a negative item that is showing up on the report. In most cases, it is easier to get a home loan than a credit card, because the house is the security for the mortgage.

The third reason for reviewing your credit report is for you to see if anything needs to be repaired or corrected for errors that may be reported. By doing this before you submit an application, you will spare yourself an inquiry and be able to have the problem corrected before the application is reviewed.

When qualifying for a refinance or mortgage, the lender will require credit reports from all three credit reporting agencies, called a "tri-merge." If you are married, both you and your spouse's credit reports will be merged into one report. It is very important that you know exactly what each bureau says about you.

The company that is running the "tri-merge" credit report will verify your Social Security number, employment, and previous inquiries. They will also do a thorough investigation on you.

If the lender determines that your FICO score is too low and you know there are errors on the report, now is the time to see if the company the lender is using for the "tri-merge" can help you with a credit-rescore. Remember, only a mortgage broker or lender can request this for you.

By raising your FICO score high enough to qualify for your purchase or refinance, you could be offered better terms for your loan and complete the transaction.

The Application

The amount of your down payment may determine the type of loan you can apply for. Whatever type of loan you apply for, the lender will look at certain criteria to qualify you. There are numerous forms to fill out, such as the initial loan application, verification of employment, verification of deposit, and numerous other disclosures.

Your loan application will require information about you and your spouse or co-borrower. A co-borrower is an individual who will purchase the property with you. You may need a co-borrower to help you qualify for the loan.

When you are completing the loan application, thoroughly complete the information requested. The lender will verify the information that you provide.

Verification of Employment

The lender sends the verification of employment form to your employer to verify where you work. Your employer or an authorized person will complete the form. The form will ask questions such as the date you began working at your current job, and how much your base or hourly pay is per month. If you also receive overtime pay, bonuses, or commissions, this must be included in the form.

The lender is looking for employment for at least two years at the same job. If a person has been employed at his or her current job for less than two years, an additional verification of employment form will be sent out to the previous employer.

If an individual has been unemployed for a period of time, the lender may have a problem with stability. A letter of explanation may be required. It would then be up to the lender to approve or disapprove the loan. Because lenders have different policies for approving a loan, you may be able to go somewhere else to get an approval.

Verification of Deposit

If you are purchasing a home, the lender or bank wants to know how much money you have in an account for your down payment. They are also looking at how long you have had the down payment money in your account. They usually want to see the money in your account for a minimum of 60 days. This is called "seasoning."

The verification of deposit form is mailed to the bank or banks where the applicant has indicated the source of down payment is. The bank must fill out the form indicating the balance and average daily balance. The bank then returns it to the lender where it becomes an important part of the package.

If you are applying for a home loan, most programs do not allow you to borrow your down payment or closing costs. If you find yourself short for the down payment, some programs will allow a relative to give you the money to complete the loan. The lender would require that you get a "gift letter" from the person who gave you the money stating the money was a gift and does not need to be repaid.

The Appraisal

In most cases, having an appraisal done on the property you want to purchase is mandatory by the lender. There is a fee that the appraiser will charge. The lender will order the appraisal for you.

The appraised value will determine what the loan to value of the property will be. The bank will only loan a percentage of the appraised value. If the property's appraisal is lower than the sales price, the lender will only make the loan based on the appraisal, not the sales price. The lender will not loan more than the appraisal price, even if the selling price was higher. If the buyers want to continue with the purchase, they would have to pay the difference between the selling price and the loan amount that they were approved for, which is based on the appraisal. If they didn't want to pay higher than the appraised value, the sale would have to be renegotiated.

Additional Paperwork

The lender may request other items as part of the application, such as:

- ✓ **Past bankruptcy.** The lender will require a copy of your discharge papers.
- ✓ **Rental or investment property.** If you own rental property, a copy of all your rental agreements with a list of the real estate owned will be required.
- ✓ **Pension or Social Security income.** You will need to give the lender a copy of your award letter. In addition, you must supply the lender with a copy of the most recent check received or bank statements showing direct deposits.
- ✓ **Divorced applicant.** A complete copy of the final divorce decree and a marital settlement, if applicable, must be given to the lender.
- ✓ **Foreclosure or short-sale.** The lender may require a letter of explanation on the circumstances as to why the foreclosure or short-sale occurred. Any related documents to support your letter should be included.

Submitting the Total Package

After the credit reports, verification of employment, verification of deposits, and appraisal are all in, the package is then ready to be submitted to the underwriter (the loan company) for a final approval.

The lenders are very strict about their loan approvals and will request additional information with the submission. They will require the last two years of your federal tax returns including the

W-2s and a copy of your last two pay stubs. In addition, they will want to see the last two months' bank statements and any other assets you may have, including 401Ks, IRAs or other investment accounts.

In you are self-employed, the lender will require a complete personal and business federal tax return for the past two years, plus a current year-to-date profit and loss statement.

SECTION IV:

PROTECTING YOUR CREDIT

15

ESTABLISHING CREDIT IN YOUR OWN NAME

Now that you have learned how to qualify for credit, it is important that husbands and wives have their own separate credit. When a couple gets married, it is very common for them to begin their lives together, establishing joint credit. Both names are on accounts that they open together, and each is responsible for repaying the debt. If something happens to one of the spouses, such as a death, the surviving spouse will not lose the account, but he or she must continue to pay on it if there is a balance owed. If a divorce takes place and the accounts were held jointly, unless the account is paid off and closed, both spouses are liable for the debt.

It is a good idea to have one or two joint accounts, as well as your own separate account.

Why Having Separate Credit Is a Good Idea

Having credit in your own name keeps your accounts separate from your spouse, but also can help if you are facing a financial crisis. It's not unusual for a couple who is facing a financial hardship to fall behind in making their payments. If you both have separate accounts and you can't make all your payments, decide which one of you is going to take the hit on your credit report for late payments. Of course, that is not your first choice, but when facing financial challenges, sometimes you have to decide whether you are going to make a mortgage or rent payment or a credit card payment. Believe it or not, sometimes people will make a credit card payment first, which may not be the best option. It is always suggested to keep a roof over your head and pay your living expenses first.

The good news is that a spouse with a separate credit card in good standing can actually help the other spouse rebuild his or her credit rating. The spouse with the good credit rating can add the spouse with the tarnished rating onto his or her credit card as a user. Before you add a spouse to the account, you must make sure that the company will report the activity on both spouses' reports. The user card should be reported on both spouses' credit reports with the good payment history. This will help rebuild the credit history on the spouse's credit report more quickly.

Shawn and Andrea's Story

Shawn and Andrea were newlyweds. They had been married less than a year when Shawn was injured in an accident. He was unable to go back to work for several months. His insurance coverage had high deductibles, so they had to pay out of pocket for the rising costs of his medical needs.

While Shawn was recovering from his injury, the medical bills began to pile up. They were not able to keep up with their living expenses, as well as the added medical bills. The creditors began calling them and demanding payments, but there wasn't enough money to go around.

Both Shawn and Andrea had separate credit card accounts. They decided to keep Andrea's credit card payments current by paying only the minimum payments while Shawn's credit cards fell delinquent.

Once Shawn recovered from his injury, he was able to go back to work. With the loss of his income they had many past-due bills to catch up with, but it was going to take time. Shawn's credit report was trashed with all the delinquent accounts. It took him more than a year to bring all of his accounts current, leaving him with a negative credit report.

Andrea was able to keep all of her accounts current during this trying time. Because she had current accounts in good standing, she was able to request a credit card for Shawn. Even though Andrea was the primary cardholder, the credit card company issued Shawn a user card.

The result of Andrea putting Shawn on her credit card allowed the good payment history to be reflected on Shawn's credit report. Shawn was able to rebuild his negative credit rating faster with the new positive entries.

Credit and the Senior Citizen

Securing credit is just as important for a senior as it is for younger individuals. Unfortunately for many seniors, credit has become a necessity. People are living longer, and with the cost of living, food, and healthcare needs rising, most seniors need some sort of credit for an emergency.

Without proper knowledge of and education about the credit system, many seniors are turned down for credit. Married senior women appear to have more problems than men. Problems can occur when a married woman was only an authorized user on a credit card issued in her husband's name. Because some credit card companies do not report activity on a user's credit report, it is not unusual for a report to show no credit history in her name.

Another problem for seniors is, if they only pay cash for their purchases, they will find it difficult to open a new line of credit because there would be no credit history found when running a credit report.

If a senior is living on a reduced salary or pension, it may be more difficult to obtain a line of credit because of insufficient income. There can be several obstacles for a senior in trying to establish credit, but there is protection under the federal Equal Credit Opportunity Act (ECOA) that states a creditor cannot deny credit or terminate any existing credit because of your age.

Creditors' Evaluation

When you apply for credit, one of the major criteria for credit approval is your ability to repay the debt. This is evaluated by your current income. If you are retired or employed part-time, this may be a concern to the credit grantor. Creditors must consider the types of income a senior receives. This would include Social Security, pensions, and other retirement benefits.

When applying for credit, you should let the creditor know about your assets or other sources of income, such as real estate, savings and checking accounts, money market funds, certificates of deposit, and stocks and bonds.

The creditor will do a check on your credit history. Make sure all accounts are listed and are being accurately reported. The same evaluation will be done in qualification for a line of credit. Income and credit history are the two primary considerations.

Death of a Spouse

Under the Equal Credit Opportunity Act, a creditor cannot automatically close or change the terms of a joint account solely because of the death of a spouse. A joint account is one for which both spouses apply and sign the credit agreement. The creditor may ask you to update your credit application or reapply. This can happen if the initial acceptance was based on all or part of your spouse's income and the creditor has reason to suspect your income is inadequate to support the line of credit.

Once a reapplication is submitted, the creditor will determine whether to continue to extend you credit or make changes on your credit limit. The creditor must give a written response on your application within 30 days. While the application is being processed, you may use your line of credit with no interruptions. If for some reason your application is turned down, you must be given the reason. Sometimes an application can be turned down if the initial acceptance was based on all or part of your spouse's income, and the income now seems inadequate. To ensure protection if a spouse dies, it is important to know what kind of credit accounts you have.

Types of Accounts

1. **An individual account.** This account is opened in one person's name. The acceptance of the application is based only on the individual's income and assets.

2. **A joint account.** This type of account is opened in two people's names. Usually it is a husband and wife. The acceptance of the application is based on the income of both people or either person. Both people are liable for any debts because both have signed the credit application.

3. **A user account.** This type of account means that two people's names appear on an account or charge card, but the account is based on the income and assets of just one of those people. That person is the primary cardholder who is legally responsible for any debts.

Know Your Rights

A joint account is the only type of account that gives protection against the account being closed because of a death. It is also a good idea to have individual credit accounts. This would protect you from any account closures.

If you feel as though you have been discriminated against in any way by a creditor who has denied you credit, you may write to the Federal Trade Commission. The letter that was sent to you turning down your request for credit will have the name and address of the FTC.

If you do decide to write, it is important that you remember and list all the facts. Make sure you have written down any oral statements or discussions that took place with the creditor. Keep copies of all letters or correspondence. Submit these copies with your letters to the federal agency.

Women and Credit

Donna, Kathy, and Jane's Stories

Donna had been using her husband's credit cards for several years. When the bills came due, she would promptly pay them on time. She decided to apply for a credit card in her name and was rejected. The creditor ran a credit report on her and there was no record found. There was no information on her credit report regarding her husband's open charge accounts.

Kathy was recently divorced and changed back to her maiden name. She had several good credit accounts in her married name, but when she applied for new credit with her maiden name, no record of her credit history was found.

Jane was 25 years old and a single woman who paid cash for all her purchases. She never established credit in her name. She did not know where to begin to get credit because she had no prior credit history.

These incidents could have been avoided if these women had planned ahead on how to establish their own credit history.

Establishing Credit

Now more than ever, women are in the workforce and can establish credit in their own names. Many married women feel they need to use their husband's credit cards and not worry about having their own cards. It is important to have credit in your own name, whether married or single. You never know when you may need it for an emergency. If something ever happened to your spouse, you do not know if you would be able to reestablish yourself in the credit world. It is especially important if the accounts were in your spouse's name. Even though you were a user of the account and paid the bills, you may not have a credit record.

The Equal Opportunity Act was designed to stop discrimination against women and credit. You may not be denied credit because you are a woman, or because you are married, single, widowed, divorced, or separated.

A good place to start when trying to see what credit history you have reported on yourself is to order a credit report from the three major credit reporting agencies. Once you have received a copy of your credit reports, see what they say about your payment history. If no payment record is found, you need to take action.

If the creditors you have made payments to in the past have failed to report the accounts on your credit report and "no record is found," you will be denied credit.

When a women is widowed, divorced, or wants credit in her name, a credit application can be denied because all her previous accounts were in her husband's name. A single woman who marries may have problems after she marries because the accounts held in her maiden name may not have been transferred to a file with her married name.

Building a Good Credit Report

Here are some guidelines for women to start building a good credit.

1. If you have had credit before under your maiden name, contact the creditor and give your new married name and pertinent information. Ask them to update their files and report it on your credit report using your married name.

2. If you have shared accounts with your husband or former husband, make sure that these creditors are reporting these accounts on your credit report. If they are not, ask them to update your report.

3. If you were married or divorced recently and changed your name, ask the creditor to change your name on

your accounts. Once these accounts are in your new name, your credit history should be updated.

4. Notify each creditor that you want accounts that you share with your husband reported on both credit reports.

Know Your Rights

Once you have established yourself with your own credit report, it will be easier for you to establish new credit in your name. This is an excellent safeguard in case of an emergency. The problem will be solved before the event even takes place.

Every woman needs to be aware of her rights when applying for credit:

1. When applying for credit, you do not have to use Miss, Mrs., or Ms. with your name.

2. Creditors cannot ask questions about birth control, or your desire to have children. They cannot assume that, by having children, your income will drop.

3. The creditor must consider any income, whether full- or part-time employment, as reported on your application. Child support and alimony payments must be considered income.

4. Creditors cannot refuse to open an account because of your sex or marital status. Some women choose to use their maiden name rather than their married name. A creditor cannot make a woman use her married name. If you are credit worthy, your husband does not need to co-sign your account. Creditors may not ask for information about your husband, provided your income is high enough, or unless your account is going to be used by your husband and he is paying for your debts, or if you live in a community property state (Arizona, California, Idaho, Louisiana, Nevada, New Mexico, Texas, and Washington), where anything that is purchased during the time of the marriage becomes community property.

If you feel you have been discriminated against because of your sex, you can file a complaint with the Federal Trade Commission. Visit *www.ftc.gov* to receive a copy of the law and learn how to file a complaint.

16

PROTECTING YOUR CREDIT DURING AND AFTER DIVORCE

Going through a divorce is something most couples don't anticipate. When they get married, most couples are planning for the "happily ever after." Sometimes things happen that can change their happily ever after to an unhappily ever after with a divorce.

Filing for a divorce can be stressful on anyone. If the right steps are not taken during this stressful time, divorcees can find themselves in a huge financial mess, not only with their bank accounts, but from the serious damage that can be done to an individual's credit rating. It is in your best interests if you are facing a divorce to make sure that your credit and good name are protected before, during, and after divorce. Having a solid understanding of the way your accounts work before the divorce begins means that a recent divorcee won't have as many pieces to pick up after the divorce is final.

Know What Accounts You Have

It is important that you know whether you have a joint account with your spouse or a "user" account, as discussed in Chapter 15.

The problem many couples have when facing a divorce is handling their joint accounts. With a joint account, both parties are responsible for any debt that is incurred on the account. A serious problem divorcing couples face with joint accounts is the possibility that one of the spouses may run up a huge bill, or stop making payments that both parties are responsible for. If payments on the account aren't made, then this could ruin both parties' credit reports.

Protecting Your Accounts

If you have an individual account and your spouse is an authorized user, you need to notify the credit card company and give authorization that you want the user card to be canceled. Because you are the primary cardholder and responsible for any charges and payments owed, you are completely within your rights to do this.

If there are joint accounts, you need to request that the account be closed immediately before any damage can be done. A bank or credit card company is not allowed to close an account simply because a married couple has divorced or are contemplating divorce. However, if one of the spouses on the card requests that the account be closed, then the lending institution is allowed to make the changes. This issue should be addressed immediately.

Closing accounts or removing authorized users gives you a better chance of keeping your credit intact and not ending up with a tarnished credit report. Credit survival and preventing future credit problems must be addressed in case things turn ugly.

Steps to Take Before the Divorce

1. Gather all of the credit card statements, monthly bank account records, student loan documents, mortgage and loan agreements, and other sources of debt you hold both individually and jointly with your spouse. Everything needs to be laid out to see how much debt is owed. You also need to determine whose debt it is, who the creditor is, the amount owed, and the date the debt occurred.

2. Decide how to divide or dispose of property. If necessary, you can use a mediator to work through this with your former spouse.

3. As previously mentioned, contact the creditors for each account that you hold jointly and request that the account be closed. Remember, even if the divorce decree names the spouse who is required to make payments on an account, if it is held jointly, this still does not release your liability for the account. That is why it is essential to close the account so no more purchases can be made. If the spouse who is required to make the payments doesn't make them or falls behind, your credit report will be affected, too.

4. Don't ever assume your soon-to-be-ex is making the payments for debt or trust these payments will be made. Unfortunately, divorce sometimes brings out the worst in people. Sometimes revenge is taken to hurt the other person by not making payments. The former spouse simply doesn't care how missing payments will impact the other person or his or her credit report.

5. Don't forget to keep up the payments on your individual debt accounts. A divorce doesn't wipe out debts you created before your divorce or those incurred before marriage.

6. Pay off as much as you can or all of your outstanding debts. This will prevent the debts from growing larger due to late payments, or disagreements over who should pay for what. This will give you a new debt-free beginning as you restructure a new life after a divorce. You may have to take out a loan to do this, or maybe a family member may step in to help.

7. If you don't have credit in your name, now is the time to establish it.

Joint Assets

A joint account that many married couples share as an asset and named on a title together could be a home, a car, bank accounts, and so on. Decisions need to be made on how these assets will be distributed between you. You may need to talk to legal counsel before making any final decisions and understand all the facts and consequences.

Your Home and Mortgage

Your home and mortgage should be your number-one priority. When a divorce occurs, it is not a good idea to walk away from a mortgage if it is in both of your names. Here are some options you may have.

✓ **Sell the home.** If possible, make sure the sale occurs before the divorce. If either one of the spouses is still living in the house during the divorce proceedings and really doesn't want to sell it, he or she can stall any showings by the realtor and drag the sale out indefinitely. In the meantime, you both are responsible for the payments and your credit may be in jeopardy.

✓ **Refinance the home in his/her name.** If one spouse wants to keep the house after the divorce, insist that the soon-to-be-ex obtain new financing in his or her own name. The current mortgage company will not remove any names from the loan just because of a divorce. If it is a joint account, until the loan is refinanced and the original lender is paid off, both parties are responsible for the payments.

Refinancing in one of your names will eliminate the title from being held jointly. The signer on the promissory note with the new lender is the only one responsible for the loan.

✓ **If selling or refinancing isn't an option.** If refinancing or selling is not something you can do, and one of you is going to continue to live in the home, you need to protect yourself.

❑ Don't take your name off the title. If you take your name off the title by using a quit claim deed, you are removing ownership, but not loan responsibility. If you do this and at a later date sell the property, you will not be able to split the equity in the home when it sells.

❑ You should have an agreement on how long your ex can stay in the house before it will be sold or refinanced.

❑ Notify the mortgage company of your change of address and have all statements and coupon booklets sent to your new address.

Bank Accounts

Any joint bank accounts, whether they are a checking account, savings account, investment account, CDs, or what, need to be addressed for both spouses' protection. The best thing to do is contact legal counsel to help you with the division of these accounts.

This needs to be done quickly because both spouses have access to the accounts and one not-so-nice spouse can drain the money.

Car Loans

Car loans are the second most important kind of financing on your credit report after your mortgage. Here are possible ways to cope with joint car ownership:

- ✓ **Sell the car.** Make sure the sale occurs before the divorce. As long as the car is not sold, you are responsible for the payments and your credit is in jeopardy. If you owe more than the car is worth, it's still better to sell the car at a loss than to risk your credit.

- ✓ **Have one spouse refinance the car in his or her own name.** If one spouse is to keep the car after the divorce, you need to have the spouse who is keeping the car obtain new financing in his or her own name.

- ✓ **If selling or refinancing isn't an option.** If selling the car is going to cause hardship to your spouse and he or she is unable to refinance the car on his or her own, here are some things you can do to protect yourself:

  - ❑ Don't take your name off the title. If you take your name off the title, you are removing ownership, but not loan responsibility. Your name is still on the loan.

  - ❑ Place a limit on how long your spouse can have possession of the car before it will be sold or refinanced.

  - ❑ Notify the lender of the car of your change of address and have copies of all statements sent to your new address.

After the Divorce

After the divorce, you will probably be mentally and emotionally drained. You may be somewhat fearful as to what the future holds. Having to support yourself and possibly being a single parent may seem overwhelming. This is especially true when it comes to managing your finances.

As you regroup and try to get your finances back in order, there are some things that you can do to help along the way. Here are some suggestions.

- ✓ **Review your credit report.** As early as possible in the divorce process, you should pull the most recent copy of your credit report from the three main credit bureaus. Visit *www.annualcreditreport.com*. Review each report to make sure that everything is accurate. Make sure the joint accounts are closed and any open balances are being paid on time.

- ✓ **Create a new budget.** As with most divorces, there is a huge shift in income for both parties. It is important that you create a workable budget based on your current income and expenses. It is going to take discipline and a new way of looking at your finances to make it work. If you need to pay for court-mandated child support or spousal support, make sure you allocate this in your budget. Remember to be very conservative in your budgeting. Try to find ways to have money left at the end of the month to put into savings.

- ✓ **Seek professional tax and financial planning advice.** Your current tax liability may have changed after the divorce. Because divorces are complicated, you need to talk with financial advisors to help you maximize your financial benefits and minimize your tax and other obligations.

- ✓ **Changing back to your maiden name.** Your credit history will not disappear if you go back to using your maiden name. If you go back to using your maiden name, contact your individual creditors to have your name changed on the accounts. The accounts will then show up under your maiden name. Remember, in addition to your name, your credit reports are matched up to your Social Security number. You must establish new credit in your own name, especially if all of your previous credit was joint credit with your spouse.

Tips on Rebuilding Credit After a Divorce

✓ As previously mentioned, be sure to cancel all joint credit card accounts.

✓ All credit accounts you had while using your married name should be changed to the name you are using now.

✓ Open a bank account in your name.

✓ The sooner you establish new accounts in your name, the faster you can rebuild your credit.

✓ If you have gone back to using your maiden name, apply for a new credit card using that name.

17

CREDIT CARD REGULATIONS

What You Need to Know

Anytime anyone hears the word *change*, there is an instant reaction of dread and concern for the unknown, especially when it has to do with your finances. The first thought that goes through your head is, "How will this affect me?"

The Credit CARD Act of 2009, also known as the Credit Card Accountability, Responsibility and Disclosure Act, was signed into law in May 2009. Changes became effective in February 2010 when the first round of provisions went into effect.

There were many changes and rules under the new credit card law, which, in actuality, was created to protect you from banks and credit card issuers. However, as with anything new, change is sometimes hard to get used to or understand. The new credit card laws can be confusing and difficult to make sense of because there are so many aspects to this novel act.

The goal of this new law was to put an end to the bad behavior and unethical practices in the credit card industry, while simultaneously improving consumer disclosures in addition to other benefits. Sounds good, right? Although there is a good side to this new law, there is a bad side that also comes along with these changes.

Why Did This Law Come About?

The government felt that change in the credit card industry was essential and long overdue, especially due to the difficult economic climate of our country. Change was needed regarding consumer protection and credit card practices.

The lawmakers wanted the credit card companies to communicate better, to be more transparent, and notify consumers of interest rate changes to their credit cards further in advance. These policymakers were concerned about the old practices of credit card companies and wanted to provide a way for consumers to repay the debt they owed, as well as to be able to access their credit.

Most of the changes created clearer communication between the credit card issuer and the consumer, reasonable fees, and more uniformity regarding interest rate increases. However, this law does not cap how high interest rates can increase and what fees that credit card issuers can collect. Let's take a closer look at how these changes will affect you.

How Will This Law Affect You?

In trying to understand the effects of this new credit card legislation, you may be wondering how this law will affect you, your current credit card and interest rates, fees, and your future ability to get credit.

Maybe you've already seen additional fees applied, your interest rate increase, or your credit limit lowered, and you don't understand how this could have happened, because this new law was supposed to help you, right? Because there was such a long period of time between when the bill was signed into law in May 2009 and when the law went into effect in February 2010, many credit card companies did increase rates and annual fees, lower credit limits, and in some cases, added a charge for low usage.

This long implementation period between when the bill was signed and when it went into effect allowed some credit card issuers to take advantage of this window of time to inform you of any changes to your account. Not all of these credit card issuers jumped in with changes to accounts. If you were one of the lucky ones not affected, be grateful. It is extremely important for you as a consumer to read all of the credit card disclosure statements that you receive from your creditor. Most people throw these disclosures in the trash without ever reading them. When their account changes, they are surprised, only to learn when they contact the creditor in a rage that they were in fact forewarned of the change to their account in the disclosure that they never read.

There is a stipulation in the law that states if your interest rates were increased on or after January 2009, then your creditor needs to evaluate the rate increase and your specific situation.

What Are the Changes?

✓ **Rate increases.** The CARD Act does not allow for an interest rate increase on existing balances unless the consumer is late 60 days or more, the promotional rate elapsed, or the variable Index rate increased.

A promotional rate, which is an offer for a lower interest rate for a specific time period, must now last for a minimum of six months, and typically rates shouldn't be raised during the first year after the credit card was issued. However, if late payments of 60 days or more occur, or if there is a change in the Index rate, then the interest rates can increase.

Review your credit card agreement and read all of the fine print to find out when your interest rate will increase, when the promotional rate expires, the length of your promotional rate, and if your card has a variable rate that is tied into an Index. Once you know the specifics of your credit card agreement, it will be easier for you to shop around for credit cards with clear terms.

✓ **What to watch out for.** Even though this new legislation allows for repricing of existing balances when you are 60 days past-due, there are some credit issuers who are not increasing interest rates on existing balances. It is important to shop around in order to find a company that does not reprice existing balances. Even though the Credit CARD Act applies to the entire credit card industry, separate companies may implement aspects differently. Before you apply for a new credit card, contact the creditor to find out its policies.

✓ **Protection.** Consumers will no longer be punished with increased rates from their creditors just because they have another unconnected account in bad standing. What this means is that if you made a late payment to one creditor, or if your credit score dropped in points, you will not receive negative effects from another creditor. This used to be the common practice under the universal default clause. Now, the creditors can only make changes to your account based on that one specific account that you have with them.

If your APR does increase, the creditor has to disclose why the interest rate was raised. If it was because you were more than 60 days late, the creditor is required to lower your interest rate once you make the minimum payments on time for six months following the delinquency. This is considered a reevaluation, and your creditor is required to participate in this according to this new law.

If creditors determine that you qualify for a rate decrease, they should lower your rate within 45 days after your evaluation. However, the Credit CARD Act does not indicate what decreased amount the consumer may qualify for when the six months of on-time payments are made.

✓ **Additional advance notice.** Creditors can raise interest rates on new balances at any time for any reason, as long as they provide a 45-day advanced notice. The old law used to only provide a 15-day advance notice.

✓ **Opt-out option.** If your credit card terms change, the creditor needs to give you the right to opt out. What this means is that you can reject the new terms of your interest rate hike or any other changes that occurred. When you reject the new terms, it won't be considered a default. It also won't require payment in full on the account immediately. Instead, it will close the account out and provide you with a repayment option of at least five years. However, watch your payment percentage, as the creditor is allowed to increase your new minimum percentage, although it cannot be more than twice your previous percentage. Before opting out, read the terms over carefully. Opting out will terminate your account, which could lead to negative credit scores.

✓ **When notification isn't necessary.** If your interest rate increases because of a 60-day or more late payment, end of promotional rate, change in the Index, or if your hardship agreement ends, your creditors do not have to provide you with advance notice. They only have to provide you with a statement as to why the rate increased.

In addition, if your creditors slash your credit limit for any reason, they do not have to provide you with an advance notice. The only time they would have to provide you with an advanced notice is if the reduction in your credit limit would penalize you by creating an over-limit fee.

- ✓ **New statements.** Creditors now have to send out your credit card statements 21 days in advance, giving the consumer more advance notice. The statements also have to include the phone number to a nonprofit credit counseling company, as well as information on how long it will take to pay off your balance.

- ✓ **Fee restrictions.** Creditors cannot charge you an over-the-limit fee unless you allow them to approve the over-the-limit transactions. If you allow the over-the-limit fee, creditors cannot charge more than one over-the-limit fee in each billing cycle. Also, the creditor is not allowed to charge fees that will push your balance beyond 25 percent of your initial credit limit. In addition, creditors and banks can no longer charge you a fee to make an expedited payment by phone or via the Internet.

  Although there are some fee restrictions, creditors are probably going to try to make up their fees somewhere else. Most likely the new fees will show up in annual fee hikes or inactivity fees. Read your statements and terms carefully.

- ✓ **Payment allocation.** Previously, when consumers transferred balances to take advantage of lower interest rates and still made new purchases, creditors were allowed to apply the minimum payment to the amount with the lowest interest rate first. This allowed creditors to benefit more from maximizing finance charges.

  Now, creditors have to apply the payment to the highest interest rate balance first, then to the succeeding balances. This benefits you, the consumer, as you will save some money being charged to you in finance charges.

✓ **Double billing.** The new credit card law ends double billing cycles. This was a technique that creditors used to make more money in finance charges. For example, if you had a $500 balance and you made a $400 payment, your next bill would still have charged you the interest rate from the original amount of the previous bill as opposed to the remaining $100 balance. The good news is with the current law, if you revolve a balance from the prior month, you will only be charged an interest rate on the remaining balance.

✓ **Rewards credit cards.** If you have a rewards credit card, there will most likely be changes to the rules and restrictions of the rewards programs. Some creditors may take reward points away if the account isn't current, and others may revoke points or rewards earned if the payment is late. Some creditors are thinking of other ideas on how to make a penny, such as charging fees in order for cardholders to get their points back.

There are definitely going to be more changes with these rewards programs, as we have already seen tighter rules for rewards credit cards. In order to not be affected by these rules, make sure you are on time with your payments. Also, check your rewards status from time to time to see when you have enough points to redeem your rewards. When you have enough points, cash your them out or redeem them for other rewards so you don't lose them.

✓ **Gift cards.** Not only do these new laws affect credit cards, but they affect gift cards, too. The new law does not allow gift cards to expire for a minimum of five years, thus protecting gift card holders. However, issuers can charge an inactivity fee once the gift card has gone unused for 12 months or more.

Opening New Credit Card Accounts

Due to all of the changes and how creditors have been limited in some of their charges, issuers are looking to make up their fees somewhere else. One of the places this is occurring is at the opening of a new account. People who initially have a good credit score are still experiencing increases in their initial interest rate. By penalizing consumers who have a good credit score with higher interest rates, they are salvaging their losses with the high-risk consumers.

In addition, those consumers with poor credit scores will most likely be denied credit, or only receive extremely low limits. Because they pose a higher risk, they will have less access to credit.

Students are also affected more by these changes, as there are tighter restrictions for consumers under the age of 21 to obtain credit. Students who cannot provide a co-signer or who do not have steady income will not be able to qualify for a credit card.

By making credit harder to access for students, the government believes they will be able to stop young people who cannot provide the means of income from getting into too much debt.

Stay Informed

It is your responsibility to stay informed on how the Credit CARD Act can affect you. Periodically do your own research on the law to see if there are any changes that may affect you and your accounts.

Many people saw firsthand and felt the impact from the creditors on their accounts during the time between when the law was signed off and when it went into effect. It gave creditors time to strategize and find ways to make other profits and offset some of their future losses. New fees have surfaced, such as an increase in initial fees, addition of inactivity fees, and other miscellaneous fees, as well as interest rate increases on new accounts.

To make sure you are not negatively affected by this new law, make sure your payments are on time, read all your credit card statements, and watch for changes.

If you are having financial problems and cannot make your credit card payments, contact your creditor to find out if you can qualify for a financial hardship or payment program. These programs typically have lower interest rates or temporarily suspend fees.

Many creditors are now suggesting that people facing these financial hardships contact a nonprofit debt management company for help. The nonprofit company I recommend is Cambridge Credit Counseling Corp. Visit: *www.cambridge-credit.org* or call: (800) 208-5084.

18

IDENTITY THEFT AND YOU

Have you ever wondered how people become victims of identity theft? Or maybe it has happened to you and you're not sure how it happened. There are many methods thieves use in order to get ahold of your personal information.

In this chapter, we are going to explore what identity theft is, how to protect your identity, common ways of identity theft, where to turn and what to do if you find yourself a victim of identity theft, plus how to rebound if it happens to you.

Identity theft is a form of fraud. It is defined as taking or assuming another person's identity in order to use existing accounts, open new credit accounts, or obtain other benefits of their personal information for a fraudulent purpose. Typically, a person's credit cards are stolen to make purchases. Also, Social Security cards and numbers have been taken in order to establish new credit in your name.

How Identity Theft Happens

Identity theft occurs in a variety of ways; thieves gain access to your personal information by stealing it out of your purse or wallet, impersonating an official representative, and stealing your information through the mail and through computer technology. Here are some of the ways that identity thieves acquire your personal information:

- ✓ **Skimming.** Sometimes, when you swipe your credit card or debit card in a normal transaction, there may be a special storage device attached to the card reader. This device captures and stores up to several hundred credit card numbers at a time. Once the information is uploaded to a computer, the identity thief has access to your information without you even knowing it.

- ✓ **Hacking.** Many identity thieves are hackers as well. They will use clever programming to break into your personal computers or computer systems in companies that have personal records on file. Some banks have even been victims of hackers, and many of their customers may have been victims of identity theft.

- ✓ **Stealing mail.** Your mail includes credit card statements, tax information, bank statements, pre-approved credit offers, and even new checks. Thieves can steal right from your mailbox and have even been known to have mail forwarded to them. This confidential information is right at their fingertips and can help them steal your identity.

- ✓ **Dumpster diving.** Identity thieves often rummage through your personal trash, which even occurs at businesses. Thieves sort through the garbage to find bank account numbers, credit card numbers, financial statements, and other personal information.

✓ **Stealing purses and wallets.** If you sit your purse or wallet down even for a second, it may be stolen by an identity thief. Most wallets and purses contain credit cards, debit cards, a driver's license, and some even contain Social Security cards. A purse or wallet is a goldmine for an identity thief. *Do not carry your Social Security card in your wallet or purse.*

✓ **Employees of businesses.** Sometimes identity thieves may steal personal records from businesses. This could be the work of an employee stealing customer records from his or her own employer to gain access to confidential information. Often, identity thieves will conspire with an employee at a company who can get them access to personal records. In addition, employees who have access to credit reports may abuse their rights to that information.

✓ **E-mails and phone calls.** Identity thieves have been known to impersonate your bank, creditor, or representative from another company by calling or e-mailing you. If you receive a suspicious phone call or e-mail asking for your personal information to either verify your account or to claim money, do not do it. Whatever the scheme, they are most likely trying to steal your credit card number, Social Security number, or other account numbers.

✓ **Home theft.** Some thieves will break into your home not to steal your television or jewelry, but to take your identity. They will steal tax information, bank account numbers, Social Security numbers, credit card account numbers, and any other personal information they can find.

What to Do If You Are a Victim of Identity Theft

Has this ever happened to you? You just received a collection notice in the mail for an account that you didn't use or even know about, you received a credit card in the mail that you never wanted or opened, or you just got turned down for a loan or credit card because of a low FICO score with accounts that weren't even yours. If one of these situations has happened, you are most likely a victim of identity theft.

You may feel robbed, violated, and left wondering how this could happen to you. Your credit scores have most likely been negatively affected. You may need a loan or credit, and this situation is making it impossible for you to obtain. You need to take control and find out what to do next in order to fix the damage that has already occurred and minimize any future harm.

There are criminal laws that govern identity theft. According to the Identity Theft and Assumption Deterrence Act of 1998 (3. 18 U.S.C. § 1028(a)(7)), it is a crime to "knowingly transfer or use, without lawful authority, a means of identification of another person with the intent to commit, or to aid or abet, any unlawful activity that constitutes a violation of Federal law, or that constitutes a felony under any applicable State or local law."

Because identity theft is a crime, there are many things that can be done if you find yourself a victim of it. The law is in place to provide a centralized complaint process for victims, as well as strengthen the criminal laws governing identity theft. If you are a victim of identity theft, you must take immediate action. The law allows victims to dispute unauthorized charges; however, there are certain time deadlines that need to be watched.

  ✓ **Notify the creditor.** If you have found unauthorized charges on your credit or debit card, you most likely have been a victim of identity theft. The good news is that the Fair Credit Billing Act limits your responsibility to $50 in unauthorized charges. Once you find the unauthorized charges, you will need to write your creditor, disputing the questionable charges.

Write the dispute letter to your creditor's "billing inquiries" department. Make sure you send the letter certified mail so that you know it reaches your creditor. Notify your creditor as soon as you spot the unauthorized charge, and make sure your letter reaches them within 60 days after the first bill that showed the error. Keep a copy of the letter for yourself. By law, your creditor has to respond within 30 days of receiving your letter, and must resolve the dispute within two billing cycles.

✓ **Notify your bank.** If your debit card was stolen, you need to report it within two business days to your bank. Under the Electronic Fund Transfer Act, you will only be held liable for $50 in unauthorized charges; however, if you report the unauthorized charges between three and 60 days, you will be responsible for $500 of unauthorized charges. If you wait until after 60 days, you may lose all the money that was stolen from your account. If your debit card has a Visa or MasterCard logo, those companies will limit your liability to $50 per card in unauthorized charges.

It is best if you notify your creditors and banks as soon as you can once you notice fraudulent charges or that your debit cards, credit cards, and even personal checks have been stolen. The longer you wait to contact your issuer, the higher the chance that you will be responsible for some or all of the unauthorized charges.

✓ **Fraud alert.** If you have been a victim of identity theft, it is important that you create a fraud alert.

When you contact the credit reporting agencies, you will have two different types of fraud alerts to chose from—the extended alert and the initial alert.

The extended alert entitles you to receive two free credit reports from each credit reporting bureau per year; however, the fraud alert will remain on your file for seven years. The most common type of fraud alert is the initial alert. This will stay on your file for 90 days and will provide you with one free credit report from each of the three reporting agencies.

In order to establish an extended alert, you must have a police report and evidence of the fraud or attempted fraud. You may request that only the last four digits of your Social Security number are visible on your credit report for your protection. Also, you may cancel a fraud alert at any time.

It is in your best interest, to set up a fraud alert for your own protection. Creditors will take more precautions when reviewing your application for credit or a loan, and you will be alerted if someone is trying to open accounts using your identification. This way the thief will not be able to open credit in your name. When you contact one of the credit reporting agencies to set up fraud alert, it must tell the other credit reporting bureaus.

Your credit report and credit score are crucial to you and your credit future. Make sure you check them often to make sure that you are not a victim of identity theft.

✓ **Police report.** It is in your best interest to file a police report if you find that you are a victim of identity theft. Some creditors may require a police report to use as proof of the incident. Some police stations are hesitant to take an identity theft report. Make sure you are persistent with your request. Make sure you keep a copy of the report for your records because credit card companies and banks may require to see the report in order to verify the unauthorized charges. Also, make sure you have the investigator's name and phone number, in case your creditors need to speak with him or her.

✓ **Social Security Administration.** If your Social Security card was taken or if you know that your Social Security number was used to open up new credit, you must contact the Social Security Administration office. Most of the time, they will issue you a new Social Security number and card. In order to apply for a new Social Security number, you need to provide evidence that you are still being hurt by someone using your card. You will need to prove your age, U.S. citizenship or lawful immigration status, and identity. For more information visit: *www.ssa.gov/pubs/10064. html#new.*

✓ **Postal inspector.** If you suspect that your mail has been stolen or that it was forwarded to a different location, you have most likely been a victim of identity theft in which a thief rummaged through your mail or used a Change of Address form to forward your mail to them. Call the postal inspector to report and have this theft investigated. They can be reached at (877) 876-2455 or *http://postalinspectors.uspis.gov.*

✓ **Department of Motor Vehicles.** If your driver's license was stolen, you need to contact your state agency that issued your license. Most of the time you can find their contact information by searching online for your state's Department of Motor Vehicles. They will cancel your license and provide you with instructions on how to obtain another one.

✓ **Federal Trade Commission.** If you have been a victim of identity theft, you should report the crime to the Federal Trade Commission (FTC). Contact them at (877) IDTHEFT or *www.idtheft.gov*. Although the FTC does not investigate identity theft, it shares the complaints with the appropriate governing agencies that help fight identity theft nationwide.

Protecting Yourself From Identity Theft

In order to prevent identity theft from happening to you, it is essential that you begin to take proactive steps immediately. Also, if you have been a victim of identity theft, it is important that you deal with the aftermath quickly to prevent any further damage.

Here are some of the proactive steps you can take to avoid becoming a victim of identity theft:

✓ **Check your mailbox.** You should check your mailbox frequently so that no mail is left in there for more than one day or overnight. You should consider getting a lock for your mailbox if your mailbox doesn't have a security feature. Also, when you go on vacation, consider having your mail held at the post office so that you don't become victim of identity theft.

✓ **Secure your computer.** Hackers use smart programming to get what they want from your computer; however, you can stop them from accessing your private information if you make your computer secure. Do not store financial information on your hard drive, and make sure your firewall is protecting your computer. Also, wireless routers allow you to create an individual password. Make sure you customize a password that includes a mixture of numbers, letters, and characters. *Do not store your passwords on your computer.*

✓ **Use a locked file cabinet.** Make sure your financial documents, Social Security cards, passports, bank statements, credit card statements, and tax information is stored in a locked filing cabinet or secured safe.

It is also a good idea to keep a list of all your credit cards and account numbers in this secured safe or locked filing cabinet. This way, if your wallet or purse ever get stolen, you will have a complete list of account numbers, creditors, and contact information to call in an emergency. Do not leave this list anywhere else besides a locked/secure location. Also, do not store your Social Security card in your wallet or purse. Keep this in your safe as well.

✓ **Shred important documents.** Do not throw away your bank statements, credit card statements, or any other financial documents. Thieves have been known to dig through people's trash looking for personal information they could use to steal their identity. Protect yourself by shredding all your important personal information instead of throwing it away.

Also, do not throw away pre-approved credit card offers, but shred them. If you want to decrease the amount of pre-approved offers you receive by mail, call (888) 567-8688 to opt out of telemarketing lists used by the three credit reporting agencies.

✓ **Check credit reports.** It is a wise idea to check your credit reports once a year. Under the Fair and Accurate Credit Transactions Act, you can receive one free credit report each year from all three of the credit reporting agencies.

Review Chapter 8 regarding what to look for when reviewing your credit reports.

19

MEDICAL IDENTITY THEFT

Most people are not aware of medical identity theft; however, it is more common than you think. By safeguarding your identification, you can avoid becoming a medical identity theft victim.

Medical identity theft occurs when another person other than yourself uses your personal information, name, and insurance information or Social Security number to receive healthcare services or medical products. It is a part of healthcare fraud, and is considered a crime. This crime makes both healthcare providers and individuals the victim, creating financial losses for both the insurers and victims, as well as life-long consequences for the victim. This is not just a crime against the healthcare system, but against individuals who may be stuck having to clean up their medical records and credit reports.

Medical identity theft isn't as widely talked about, as it doesn't occur as frequently as financial identity theft. Medical theft can cause great harm to victims because it leaves a trail of false information in medical records that can affect victims' financial and medical futures.

You may first learn of the problem through a debt collector looking to get paid on a past-due medical bill. You may think there has been a mistake, but once you look a little further, you realize that someone has taken your identity to seek medical treatment and services or to obtain products. You may not know where to turn or what to do if you find yourself a victim of medical identity theft.

Protecting Yourself From Medical Identity Theft

Discovering medical identity theft can be hard, unless you get that call from a debt collector. Others find out when an insurance investigator tells them of a problem or concern. Because it is harder to find, here are some proactive steps you can take and different areas you can look into:

- ✓ **Monitor Explanation of Benefits statements.** Carefully review your insurance statements. If you notice inaccurate information, such as charges for services you did not receive, charges for medical equipment you did not use, or charges for office visits you did not make, then you should contact your insurer or provider.
- ✓ **Credit report.** Some victims of medical identity theft have found a collection notice for a medical bill or hospital bill on their credit reports.
- ✓ **Medical records.** Under the health privacy rule issued under the Health Insurance Portability and Accountability Act (HIPAA), you have the right to get a copy of your medical records from each healthcare provider. This includes records from hospitals, doctors' offices, pharmacies, or even laboratories. Inspect the

files to make sure that there are no inaccuracies and that you are not a victim of medical identity theft.

Asking for all your health records may be overwhelming and give you too much information to sort through. If you are questioning a certain incident or bill you received or were notified about, then you should ask for that specific record. Getting information on that one specific incident will most likely provide you with the information you need; however, if you still have additional questions, you can always ask to see more of your medical records.

Although you have a right to request your medical files, sometimes they are difficult to obtain. Some hospitals or doctors will charge you for copies, and others might be reluctant to show you health records and may reject your request. If you are being denied access to your medical files, you can file an appeal.

If you decide to file an appeal of the denial, you can find the appeal procedure for your specific provider under your provider's privacy policy or notice of privacy practices. If you request a copy of the privacy policy, your healthcare provider is required to provide you with a free copy.

If you find that your healthcare providers are not cooperating with your request and you feel that it is too difficult to view your medical file or receive a copy of your medical records, you may file a complaint with the Department of Health and Human Services' Office of Civil Rights at (800) 368-1019 or *www.hhs.gov/ocr/*.

What to Do If You Are a Victim of Medical Identity Theft

Once you discover that you have been a victim of medical identity theft, you may be confused about where to turn to get help and what you should do first. Whatever you do, do not ignore the problem. What if your file said you had a surgery that you never had, a disease, or even a different blood type? Having incorrect information in your permanent medical file could have serious consequences for your future, making it difficult to obtain future health coverage or life insurance. Here are some helpful tips on what to do after you have been victimized:

- ✓ **Police report.** It is essential to file a police report if you are a victim of medical identity theft. Many times, victims of medical identity theft will suffer financial impacts, as collections from hospitals or medical bills may be listed on credit reports. A police report is helpful to provide to insurance companies and healthcare providers regarding this crime.

  Keep a copy of this report for yourself, and send it to insurers, credit bureaus, and providers as it will help in your efforts to get your medical records cleaned up.

- ✓ **Correct false information.** If you are a victim of medical identity theft, you need to make sure that you don't just clean up your financial mess, but that you clean up your medical records, too. It can be a lengthy process, but you don't want incorrect information in your permanent medical records. Request that the false information be removed from your medical file, especially if there is incorrect information listed in your file, such as a disease that you do not have.

  Hospitals and doctors are sometimes hesitant to correct or remove information from a medical record.

You may need to explain what happened and what is wrong with your medical file, show them the police report, or seek legal help if you aren't getting anywhere.

However, do not just stop with having your doctor's office delete the incorrect information from your file. If they have this inaccurate information, your insurance company most likely does as well. You need to contact your insurance provider and make the same requests to amend your health records. Under the HIPAA federal health privacy rule, when you make a request from one record keeper, it has an obligation to inform those to whom the original information was disclosed. However, do not rely entirely on them to correct all your medical records.

Unfortunately, you may have to call many different places, such as pharmacies and laboratories, and speak with record keepers to make the same requests or to make sure that they received the updated corrections. This can be a huge project and extremely time intensive, but don't give up.

✓ **Accounting of disclosures.** Under HIPAA, you have a right to get a copy of the accounting of disclosures (also known as the history of disclosures) that providers or insurers have made. This shows what information was disclosed, when, why it was released, and who received this information. This information will be a helpful tool to you in combating medical identity theft. It will allow you to know who received this information and where it went, making the tracking process easier.

✓ **Credit report.** You may have discovered that your credit report shows a collection notice for a laboratory bill or other medical bill that isn't yours. In order to remove this incorrect information from your credit report, send your police report to the collection agency and place a dispute on the collection notice. Send a letter to the three credit reporting agencies with a copy of your police report, letting them know you were a victim of medical identity theft.

✓ **Compare files.** In some cases, victims of medical identity theft were able to compare their regular, older medical files to dismiss the incorrect entries. For example, if the thief who used your personal information had a surgery that you didn't, a disease, or a different blood type, older files could prove that the debt doesn't belong to you, and that the information in your file should be removed. Also, the thief may be younger or older, which could help prove your innocence.

Helpful Information for Medical Identity Theft Victims

If you suspect that you have been a victim of medical identity theft, there are some important phone numbers and Websites you should contact.

✓ Inspector General of Health and Human Services: Fraud Hotline (800) HHS-TIPS or (800-447-8477).
✓ Federal Trade Commission (FTC): Theft Hotline (877) IDTHEFT or (877-438-4338). Or, *http:// www.consumer.gov/idtheft/*
✓ Your own insurer: Call your insurer and ask for the fraud hotline.

The Federal Trade Commission Website is a helpful site for reviewing more prevention tips and procedures for the aftermath of medical identity theft. Review the proper procedures under the Fair Credit Billing Act at *www.ftc.gov/bcb/conline/pubs/credit/fcb. htm.* Also, the Blue Cross/Blue Shield Website has helpful information and tips for medical identity theft and preventing fraud.

They recommend that you treat your medical card as thought it's as valuable as a credit card. If it is lost or stolen, you should report it to your insurer and provider, as it could be used to gain services and drugs. Visit: *www.bcbs.com/antifraud/*.

If you have been a victim of medical identity theft, you may also get assistance from fraud investigators, lawyers, and some states even have health departments that give assistance in these types of matters. Just remember, although this process can be exhausting and overwhelming, it is extremely important that you get the false information removed from your medical records.

Always be aware of anyone who has a copy of your medical identification card, as well as your Social Security number and other identification. Never assume you are safe with your identification—you never know who is lurking in the shadows.

CONCLUSION

As you have read, there are so many ways for you to rebuild and jump back into the credit arena after taking a fall. The problem that people tend to have when rebuilding is that there is always that hidden temptation to revert back to old habits. The thought that may go through your head when you are contemplating making a purchase may be, "I'll just use my credit card this one time." Don't do it! It is the one time that will release the old self to start charging again.

You have worked hard to get to this point with reestablishing and repairing your credit. It wasn't an overnight happening, but you are now in a place where you should be worry-free.

Keeping your credit and finances in order is a life-long process. With dieting, they say is it a lifestyle change, and the same is true for our finances. By changing your lifestyle and living within your means, you will not only feel good about your situation, but you can also be an example to your family and friends. Kids learn how to handle finances by the examples of their parents. If you are a good money manager, chances are, your children will be when they are adults. Even if you fell on hard times, your children will be watching how you picked yourself up.

One important thing to take away from this book is to make sure you have a workable budget. This can't be stressed enough. It's stepping out of your budget and not keeping tabs on what is coming in and going out that will set you back. It's a new habit worth learning.

There are new laws and regulations that are constantly changing. Part of your new financial life is to stay on top of any new changes. Always read the disclosures you receive from your bank and credit card companies. Even the tiny fine print that you can barely read holds information that can change the terms of your credit and cost you more money.

In today's society, you can't be too careful with your personal identification. It's too bad we have to be on the lookout for unscrupulous people who are looking to steal our identities and use them in all the wrong ways. Be on the lookout at all times in protecting you and your family's identification.

Go ahead and give yourself a pat on the back. You deserve it. You are now back on your feet and have learned from your mistakes. It's time to start moving toward your successes.

RESOURCES

Debt Management & Credit Counseling

Professional Credit Counselors, Inc.: Provides budget counseling, counseling in credit restoration, debt relief and getting out of debt, establishing credit, and more. (888) 838-4768 or *www.financialvictory.com*

Cambridge Credit Counseling: Cambridge can help you reduce your monthly payment, lower your interest rates, consolidate bills, and negotiate with your creditors: (800) 208-5084 or *www.cambridge-credit.org*

Credit Reporting Agencies

Free Annual credit report: (877) 322-8228 or *www.annualcreditreport.com*

Equifax: (800) 685-1111 or *www.equifax.com*

Experian: (888) 397-3742 or *www.experian.com*

TransUnion: (800) 888-4213 or *www.transunion.com*

FICO Scores

FAIR ISAAC: Source for FICO score and tips on improving it. *www.myfico.com*

Support for Compulsive Spenders

Debtors Anonymous: Support group in recovering from compulsive spending. *www.debtorsanonymous.org*

Financial Advisor

Hal McNaughton: 401K rollovers, investments, IRAs, and retirement planning. (800) 281-2979

Mortgages & Loans

Legacy Financial Services: Pre-qualifications for: Refinances, debt consolidation, equity loans, reverse mortgages, and purchases. (877) 740-3328 or *www.legacymoney.com*

Fannie Mae: Provides mortgage guidelines. *www.fanniemae.com*

Freddie Mac: Provides mortgage guidelines. *www.freddiemac.com*

FHA Loans

U.S. Department of Housing and Urban Development *www.hud.gov*

Real Estate

A real estate broker will assist in the purchase or sale of home or property. Call Financial Victory Institute for a referral. (888) 838-4768

Financial Websites

www.bankrate.com: Provides a list of banks and tools and information to help consumers make financial decisions.

www.cardweb.com: An online publisher of information pertaining to all types of payment cards.

Insurance

Insurance Information Institute: Directory of insurance organizations, carriers, agents, brokers, and news links. *www.iii.org*

Medicare: (800) MEDICARE (633-4227) or *www.medicare.gov*

Medicaid: Contact your state health department for information. *www.cms.hhs.gov*

COBRA: Offers extended insurance coverage. *www.dol.gov*, or contact your Human Resources Department.

Government Agencies

U.S. Department of Housing & Urban Development (HUD): Contact your local HUD office for more information. *www.hud.gov/localoffices.cfm*

Office of Child Support Enforcement: Contact state child support to inquire on reducing child support payment. *www.acf. hhs.gov/programs/cse*

Social Security Administration, Social Security Disability Insurance, and Supplemental Security Income: (800) 772-1213 or *www.ssa.gov*

Workers' Compensation: Contact your state government office to find out about workers' compensation laws and programs.

Unemployment Benefits: Contact your state unemployment office for laws and programs in your state. *www.workforcesecurity. doleta.gov*

Federal Trade Commission: (877) FTC-HELP (382-4357) or *www.ftc.gov*

Laws

Federal Trade Commission: For information on the following laws, please call the number provided or visit the provided links on the FTC Website:

- ✓ Fair and Accurate Credit Transactions Act: *www.ftc. gov/bcp/menus/consumer/credit/rights.htm*
- ✓ Fair Credit Reporting Act: *www.ftc.gov/bcp/conline/ pubs/credit/fcra.htm*
- ✓ Fair Credit Billing Act: *www.ftc.gov/bcp/conline/ pubs/credit/fcb.htm*
- ✓ Credit Repair Organizations Act: *www.ftc.gov/os/ statutes/croa/croa.htm*
- ✓ Fair Debt Collection Practices Act: *www.ftc.gov/os/ statutes/fdcpa/fdcpact.htm*
- ✓ Equal Credit Opportunity Act: *www.ftc.gov/bcp/con-line/pubs/credit/ecoa.htm*

Truth in Lending Act: (877)ASK-FDIC (275-3342) or *www.fdic.gov/regulations/laws/rules/6500-1400.html*

INDEX

ABOUT THE AUTHOR

Deborah McNaughton is the president and founder of Professional Credit Counselors, Inc. She is a nationally known credit expert and financial coach who has been in the business for more than 25 years. Deborah has been interviewed on hundreds of radio and TV talk shows including *CNN*, *Good Day New York*, *Bloomberg*, and others.

Deborah is a monthly money and financial columnist for the *Orange County Register*, and was a former radio host for the *Money Manager Show*. She has been featured or quoted in the *Los Angeles Times*, the *New York Times*, the *Wall Street Journal*, the *Chicago Tribune*, *Parade*, *Woman's Day*, *Woman's World*, and hundreds more publications.

Deborah's business offers assistance in credit consulting, mortgages, and financial planning. She is the author of several books on credit, including *Money Trouble: Surviving Your Financial Crisis*; *Rich and Thin: Slim Down, Shrink Debt & Turn Calories into Cash*; *The Get Out of Debt Kit*; *All About Credit: Questions and Answers to the Most Common Credit Problems*; *The Insider's Guide to Managing Your Credit*; and *Financially Secure: An Easy to Follow Money Program for Women.*

Deborah also offers two business opportunity manuals: *The Credit Repair System* and *Credit and Financial Strategies: Becoming a Credit Consultant*, a business opportunity manual that has helped hundreds of credit counseling businesses throughout the United States get started. Deborah conducts Credit and Financial Strategies seminars nationally and offers a distributor program for her seminars.

Deborah has educated and empowered thousands of people through her counseling, books, seminars, interviews, and newsletters regarding how to take control of their finances.

To receive more information about Deborah's seminars, products, and services, contact her at:

Deborah McNaughton

417 Associated Rd. #A102

Brea, CA 92821

Website: *www.financialvictory.com*

Phone number: (714) 993-1171